Royal Commission on Historical Monume

YORK CASTLE

Her Majesty's Stationery Office · London ·

PREFACE

This historical account of York Castle and of its buildings is off-printed, retaining the page and plate numbers, from the Royal Commission's second inventory of the monuments of the City of York—*The Defences* (1972). That volume deals mainly with the mediaeval walls surrounding the city and with their gateways and towers, but also includes the minor castle of the Old Baile and the defences of St. Mary's Abbey. York Castle itself was founded by William I adjoining the already ancient city defences. Its rebuilding in stone by Henry III in 1245–60 was followed by the construction of the present walls of York in place of wooden palisades. In modern times it has served chiefly as a prison and now houses a museum.

The opportunity is taken to mention here some additional facts which were not included in the text. Evidence of the condition of the Castle in 1308 is recorded in a document relating to twenty-one Templars who could not be imprisoned in damaged and roofless buildings there but for whom the Sheriff of Yorkshire had to rent a house in the city (PRO E358/18 rot. 33(1) under 'vadia fratrum' and *CCR 1307–13*, 33). The small early nineteenth-century stone water mill which stands beside the Foss south-east of the bailey wall was only re-erected in this position during 1964–5 and comes from Raindale, Newton, in the North Riding. Lists of stores in Clifford's Tower like that on pages 178–9 also survive in York City Archives for the years 1669–71 (Acc. 104 M/3). The occasion and surveyor of the plan of York by James Archer and that of the Castle reproduced on Plate 62 are examined in greater detail by R. M. Butler in the *Antiquaries Journal* for 1972 (LII, 320–9). The Court building has since January 1972 housed not Assizes but a Crown Court. The figures on its pediment are by John Fisher and the plasterwork by James Henderson, both of York. In the Debtors' Prison a S. window to the condemned cell has recently been unblocked and the two main staircases have been renewed.

For co-operation in the work of producing this account the Commissioners are indebted to the Corporation of York, the Department of the Environment and the Yorkshire County Committee, the owners or custodians of the constituent buildings. The City Engineer, Mr. R. A. Mayo, and Messrs. J. Nursey and W. Slater of his department have helped with information and access to office records. Assistance was also given by the Rev. E. Hudson, Vicar of St. Hilda's, Tang Hall, by Mr. J. A. S. Ingamells, Curator of the City Art Gallery, and by Mr. R. Patterson, Curator of the Castle Museum. For permission to copy or use original drawings thanks are due to York City Art Gallery (Plates 2 and 3), the Victoria and Albert Museum (Plate 7), Messrs. Brierley, Leckenby, Keighley and Groom (Plate 10 and figures on pages 62, 80, 81 and 85), and the Earl of Dartmouth and Staffordshire County Record Office (Plate 62).

The investigation into the Castle's history and structure was carried out by members of the Commission's executive staff. Dr. R. M. Butler edited the text and, with the late Mr. J. Radley, studied the mediaeval buildings. Dr. E. A. Gee and Mr. J. E. Williams were responsible for the accounts of the eighteenth-century buildings. The photographs were taken by Mr. C. J. Bassham (except for Plate 1 by Aerofilms) and the drawings illustrating the text are by Messrs. W. Masiewicz and R. F. Meads.

CASTLE YARD, YORK, AFTER LITHOGRAPH BY F. BEDFORD, 1841.

YORK CASTLE (Pls. 1–16, 62, Figs. pp. 62, 63) consists of a Norman motte and bailey with a 13th-century quadrilobate stone keep (Clifford's Tower) on the motte and remains of the mediaeval curtain wall and towers round part of the bailey, which now contains the Debtors' Prison of 1701–5, the Assize Courts of 1773–7, and the Female Prison of 1780 and 1803. The two prison buildings now belong to the City of York and house the Castle Museum.

During the past nine centuries the castle has been, like the Tower of London, a fortress, a royal palace, a mint, and a prison, as well as a court of justice and an administrative centre for the county. As a fortress it became obsolete in the 16th century, but the keep was again so used from 1642 to 1684. Its use as a palace was abandoned in the 15th century and the mint was transferred to St. Leonard's Hospital in 1546. It only ceased to be a prison in 1929 and still contains the courthouse for the North and East Ridings. For short periods in the 13th and 14th century it housed the royal treasury and courts, moved from Westminster for convenience in the wars with Scotland. In other ways too it can claim similarity with the Tower of London, for in the 18th century it contained tame deer and a raven as the Tower contained ravens and the royal menagerie. Executions took place here from 1802 to 1896 and intermittently before then of state prisoners, like Lord Clifford and Aske. (P.S. *see* p. 176.)

The site is the N.W. tip of a spur of clay between the rivers Ouse on the W. and Foss on the E., a feature which no doubt gave the name Nessgate to the street later leading to it. In the Roman period this area had been occupied by a cemetery.[1] The Roman ground surface, about 30 ft. above sea level, was overlaid by a bed of marl of varying thickness, apparently deposited by floods and containing a 'wooden boatstay . . . with

[1] RCHM, *York City*, I, 69.

an iron nail sticking into it'.[1] There is evidence elsewhere in York for severe flooding up to a level of 35 ft. above Ordnance Datum during the 5th and 6th centuries. After this periodic flooding had ceased the site of the castle was again used as a cemetery and probably also for houses beside the old Roman road of which the line is perpetuated by Coney Street, Ness Gate, and Castlegate. A new crossing of the Foss existed at the Norman Conquest on the site of the present Foss Bridge leading to a suburb where by 1100 there were at least five churches beside Fishergate. There may perhaps still have been a crossing of the Foss at or near the Roman one. St. Mary Castlegate, a pre-Conquest minster church, served the inhabitants of the castle site. Finds indicating Saxon and Viking occupation include a bronze hanging bowl, pottery loom weights, and a bone trial piece.[2]

William I built the first castle in 1068 as a motte and bailey, but it was destroyed by the Danes in September 1069 and rebuilt before the end of that year.[3] One of the seven shires of the city was laid waste for castle building.[4] The new castle was protected on the S.E. by a damming of the Foss to form the king's fishpond or stew which caused the loss of two new mills and nearly a carucate (about 150 acres) of arable, meadows, and gardens.[5] Access to Fishergate was then by a lane skirting the castle on the W. and crossing by the dam, a route known to have existed in the 12th century.

In 1070 an extension to the castle caused the destruction of a house.[6] In the 12th century there are references to the castle gate and a gaol within the castle as well as to the 'turris'.[7] In 1190 the castle ('turris Eboraci, arx regia') was burnt down in an anti-Jewish riot, killing the Jews who had taken refuge there, and rebuilt again in timber.[8] A reference to the old castle led Drake to assume that the Old Baile was involved.[9]

During the 12th and early 13th centuries features of the castle explicitly mentioned are the mound, tower, palisades, gatehouse, stone bridges, houses, stables, and gaols, including one for Irish prisoners, mentioned in 1210. Pits dug in 1192 may have been graves.[10] There was also a prison for women, apparently with a chapel above it, built by John Piper of Middleham, a priest, between 1237 and 1241.[11] Lands in the East Riding were held at this time by the service of providing an archer or crossbowman at the castle, in one case specified as within a certain tower. Lands in York and Low Hutton were similarly connected with the custody of the castle gate, and when the gate was destroyed in 1228 custody of the king's hall was substituted.[12] This destruction probably involved the tower on the motte, since it was caused by high winds.[13]

After a visit in 1244 Henry III decided to rebuild the whole castle in stone. Some work in stone had been carried out in 1200–4,[14] but most of the fortifications must still have been of wood. Over £2,450 was spent during the 20 years following this decision: Clifford's Tower, the bailey walls, towers, gates, bridges, two halls, a chapel, a kitchen, and a prison in the bailey were all apparently built at this time. Henry de Reyns, master mason, and Master Simon, carpenter, were sent to view the castle in March 1245 and arrange how it should be built. The sheriff was to consult with them and other experts and have it strengthened according to their advice.[15]

This rebuilding may have caused the abandonment of a former bailey to the W. In 1268 the Franciscan Friars, established in York by 1236, probably on the nucleus of their precinct between the castle and the Ouse, were allowed to enclose a ditch of the king's domain adjoining their area on the E. and between their area and the bridge of the bailey. They were to enclose it with an earth wall up to 12 ft. high and use it for public preaching but in wartime give up the ditch for the defence of

---

[1] YPSR (1902), 71.

[2] *Reliquary* n.s. (1906), 60; *Antiquity*, VI (1932), 166; *Med. Arch.*, II (1958), 82–3; *Ant. J.* XIX (1939), 85–90, XX (1940), 285–7; *YAJ*, XXXIV (1939), 112–13.

[3] *Two Saxon Chronicles Parallel*, I, 202; Ordericus Vitalis, *Historia Ecclesiastica*, ed. Le Prevost, II, 188, 192–5.

[4] 'vastata in castellis', Domesday Book in VCH, *York County*, II 191.

[5] *ibid.*, 193; *see below* p. 137.

[6] *ibid.*, 192.

[7] *Pipe Rolls, 1165–6*, 36; *1172–3*, 2; *1182–3*, 57; *1188–9*, 90.

[8] *William of Newburgh* (R.S. 82), I, 312–34; *Pipe Rolls, 1190*, 58, 59; *1191*, 61; *Benedict of Peterborough* (RS)II, 107.

[9] Drake, 266; *Roger of Hovedene* (RS 51), III, 34: 'et praecepit firmari castellum in veteri castellaria quod rex Willelmus Rufus ibi construxerat'.

[10] Cooper (1911), 23–32.

[11] *Close Rolls 1234–7*, 502; *CLR, 1240–5*, 40.

[12] VCH, *York*, 521–2; Widdrington, 263–4; *Close Rolls 1234–7*, 499: 'custodiam aule regis Eboraci, pro custodia janue castri Eboraci quam ipse [Johannes Doget] habere consuevit antequam predictum castrum esset prostratum'.

[13] Pipe Roll E372/73: 'pro mairemio castri Ebor. prostrato per ventum colligendo 2s.'

[14] *Pipe Rolls 1200*, 101–2; *Close Rolls 1204*, 46.

[15] *CCR, 1242–7*, 293: 'Rex mittit usque Ebor' magistrum Simonem carpentarium et magistrum Henricum cementarium ad videndum situm castri regis ibidem, et ad ordinandum et disponendum qualiter castrum quod de novo rex ibidem firmare proposuit, melius et competencius firmari possit, et mandatum est Vicecomiti Eboraci quod, assumptis secum aliis magistris in consimilibus scienciis expertis, una cum ipsis accedit, ad videndum situm ejusdem castri et qualiter illud securius et melius possit firmari, et secundum ordinationem et dispositionem eorum castrum predictum firmari faciat.'

the castle.[1] In 1280 the friars were permitted to enclose a street 130 yds. long,[2] and in 1290 to enclose a lane leading from the highway (no doubt Castlegate) to the lane leading to the mills near the castle provided they replaced it with another lane of the same size.[3] These extensions of the friary bounds indicate a shifting of the line of Castlegate Postern Lane, later widened and renamed Tower Street, from a position further N.W. In 1296 a tenement which the Friars held was described as in 'le Baill' near ('versus') York Castle.[4]

To the S. and S.E. of the castle stood the dam, which held back the fishpond, the Castle Mills, and St. George's Chapel. Although all have now disappeared they are significant in the history of the castle area. The dam was constantly in need of repair. Washed away by floods in 1315, it was rebuilt in 1316,[5] and repairs were carried out in 1320, 1324, 1328, 1335, 1379, and 1428–9.[6] A contract for work there and at the gaol made in 1377 with two carpenters is printed by Salzman.[7] In February 1643 a cut to take water from the pool to fill the city ditch beside Fishergate Postern caused a breach in the dam. Although repaired soon afterwards with piles and boards the damage remained serious and the gap was not completely closed until April 1645.[8] The dam was altered in the making of the Foss Navigation in 1797 and removed in 1856.

The Castle Mills, first mentioned in about 1135, were soon afterwards granted to the Knights Templar. On the suppression of the Order they came into the king's possession in 1312 and in 1464 were granted to St. Leonard's Hospital. At the dissolution of the Hospital they were retained by the Crown until 1570 and soon afterwards were part of the endowments of Sir Thomas Hesketh's Hospital at Heslington. After severe damage by an explosion in 1643 when used to grind gunpowder, they were rebuilt in 1650, perhaps on a slightly different site, and in 1778 equipped with a steam engine. They were finally demolished in 1856.[9]

St. George's Chapel N.W. of the mills also belonged to the Templars but in 1311 became a royal free chapel, later being used by the Guild of St. George incorporated in 1446. The chapel, together with St. George's Field, formerly the Holmes, was granted to York Corporation in 1548 and largely demolished in 1566 when the stonework was used to repair Ouse Bridge. It was rebuilt in 1576 as a half-timbered building on the mediaeval stone footings and used as a House of Correction and later as tenements, one being the Windmill Inn. The building was pulled down in 1856 but a stone shield carved with St. George's cross from above an entrance is in the Yorkshire Museum.[10]

A flood in 1315, as well as destroying the mills and dam, 'softened the soil of the motte', or perhaps 'of the moat',[11] also weakening 262 ft. of the S.W. wall of the bailey which by 1326 required fourteen buttresses.[12] In September 1319 the sheriff was ordered to man the castle, since the Scots had entered the county and lay in wait for the city and castle.[13] A tower, perhaps the keep, had been repaired to house Queen Isabella in 1327.[14] In 1333 an exchequer for Queen Philippa was made on the N. side of the bailey; palings around the king's exchequer and a wooden bridge near the S. gate were made at this time.[15] In 1360 the keep was cracked from top to bottom in two places, the vaults of the great gate and of the 'Boretour' were also cracked, the W. angle turret had partly collapsed and the great hall was ruinous since timber from its tiled roof had been taken to repair the dam;[16] the restoration carried out between 1360 and 1365 cost some £800.[17] The Exchequer and royal courts of justice had been housed in the castle intermittently from 1298 to 1392, and on several occasions the keep had held the Treasury.[18] The Chancellor of the Exchequer and some of his staff were, however, housed in St. Mary's Abbey, while the king often lodged in the Franciscan Friary. There was also a mint in the castle, rebuilt in 1353 and 1423–4[19] but moved in 1546 to the buildings of the former St. Leonard's Hospital which was in consequence known as Mint Yard.[20]

---

1 *CPR, 1266–72*, 260–1.
2 *CPR, 1272–81*, 395.
3 *CPR, 1281–92*, 332.
4 *CPR, 1292–1301*, 208; YASRS, XXI, 46.
5 *CCR, 1313–18*, 262.
6 *CCR, 1318–23*, 175; *1323–7*, 52; *1333–7*, 154; PRO LTR Foreign Accounts, E364/14m. H.; *CPR, 1464*, 335.
7 *Building in England*, 453–4.
8 B35, f. 132v; Yarburgh Muniments: Sir Thomas Hesketh's Hospital Register, ff. 8, 8v.
9 Cooper (1911), 116–32.
10 Cooper (1911), 133–140.
11 *CCR, 1313–18*, 262–3: 'terram mote illius demollivit'.
12 PRO Chancery, Misc. Inq. C 145/102(13).
13 *CCR, 1318–23*, 156.
14 PRO Pipe Rolls, E372/173 rot. 42d, quoted by Cooper (1911). 67–70.
15 *CCR, 1333–7*, 154.
16 *CIM* III, *1348–77*, 130–2 no. 366.
17 PRO Pipe Rolls, E372/205 rot. 6d; 36 Ed. III *rot. comp.* 13; 38 Ed. III rot. 9d; 39 Ed. III rot. 7d: Chancellor's Roll E352/152 *rot. comp.* 5; E101/501/11; E101/598/4–6.
18 D. M. Broome in A. G. Little and F. M. Powicke (ed.), *Essays in Mediaeval History presented to T. F. Tout* (1925), 291–300; PRO Exchequer KR E159/71/41d; Pipe Roll E372/145 rot. 19d; E372/161 rot. 9d; E372/164 rot. 29d; E372/167 rot. 31; E372/173 rot. 78; *CCR, 1318–23*, 417; *1327–30*, 162; *1392–6*, 16, 26; PRO Foreign Accounts 16 Ric. II, rot. H.
19 *CPR, 1350–4*, 513; *CCR, 1349–54*, 555; E101/598/31–2.
20 *Acts of the Privy Council*, I (1542–1547), 405.

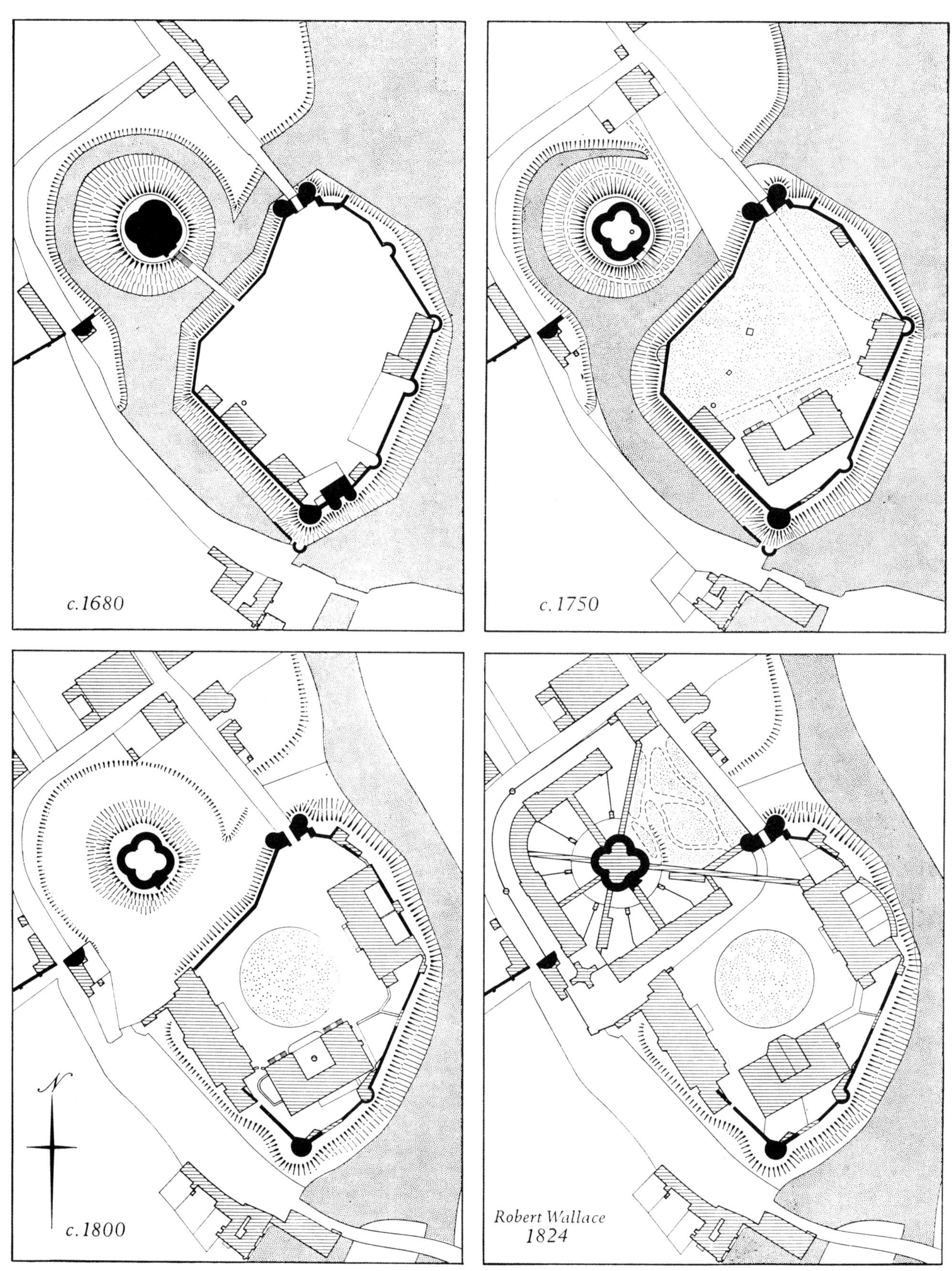

YORK CASTLE : ACTUAL AND PROJECTED DEVELOPMENT

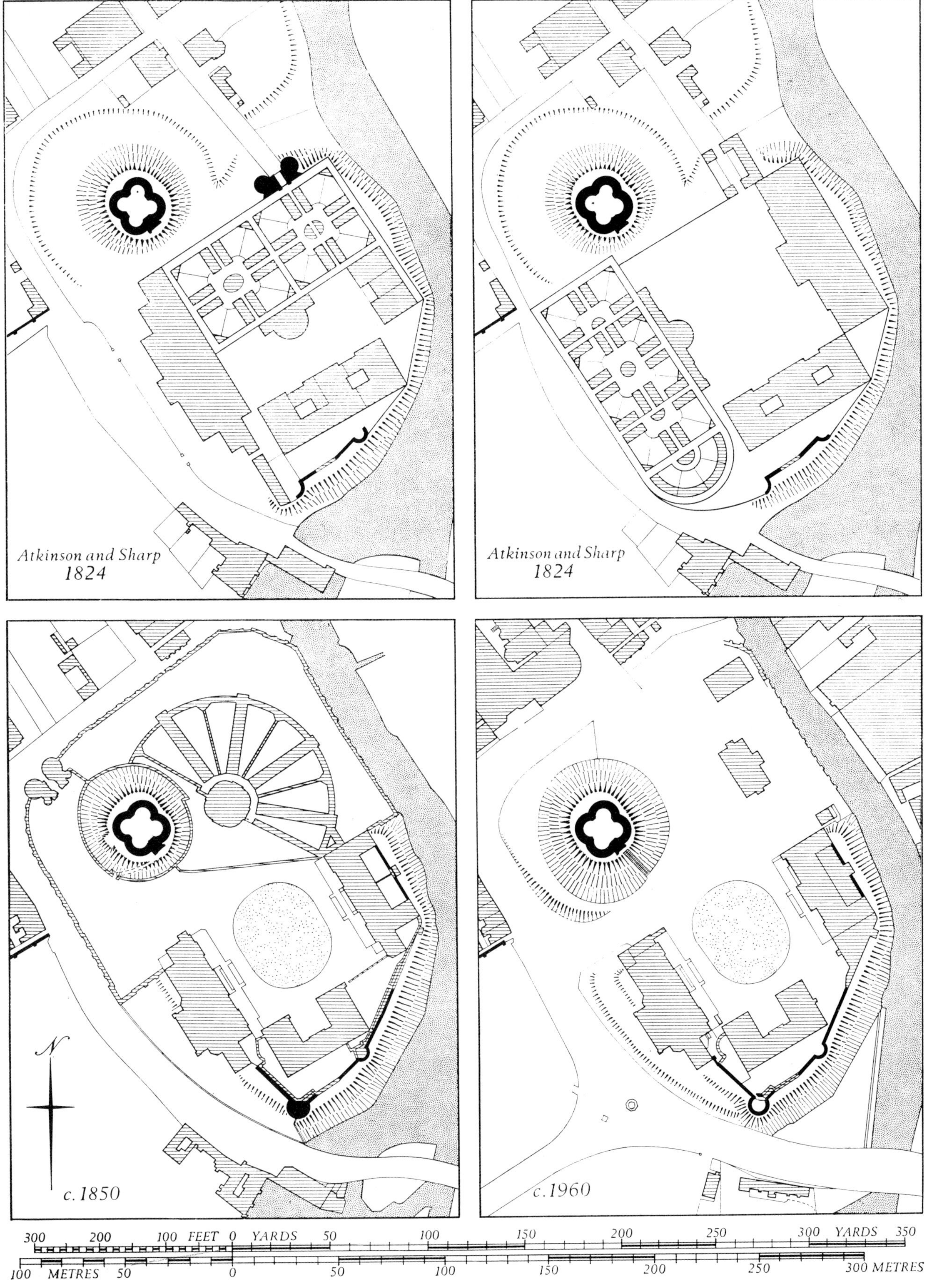

Atkinson and Sharp
1824
Atkinson and Sharp
1824
N
c.1850
c.1960
300
200
100
FEET
0
YARDS
50
100
150
200
250
300
YARDS
350
100
METRES
50
0
50
100
150
200
250
300 METRES

Many details of the structure and fittings of the castle buildings in the 14th century are known from records of expenditure. Partitions were made for the king's wine cellar in 1327 and 43,000 nails of twelve types were bought in the same year.[1] Flails on the castle gate (swivelling bars on the inside) were mentioned in *c.* 1353, and in 1364–5 wall-tiles and two great stones and iron bars for the hoods were bought for the kitchen fireplaces, the lead roof of the turret by the chapel was repaired and six weeks were spent in ramming and strengthening the dam.[2] Fittings of the Exchequer in 1320 included two counters made of fir boards and strengthened with oak and alder wood, measuring 13 ft. by 12 ft. and 11 ft. by 8 ft.[3]

Edward IV stayed in the castle, and Dodsworth ascribed to him work near Castlegate Postern,[4] but in 1484 Richard III partly dismantled the castle, preparing to rebuild it, although apparently no work was carried out.[5] By about 1535 the castle was described as in ruins both by Leland and one of Cromwell's correspondents.[6] Repairs to the castle in 1556 cost £40 and required thirty oak trees.[7] Money was collected by the county justices between 1579 and 1584 for repairs to the Moot Hall, gatehouse, and bridge.[8] Some idea of the arrangements of the prison at this time is given by narratives of recusant prisoners.[9] In 1596 Robert Redhead, the gaoler, demolished a flanking wall, probably on the W. of the bailey, the bridge to the motte, and part of Clifford's Tower itself but was stopped from further destruction by protests from the citizens.[10] In 1608 a further £243 was collected in the county to repair the new hall and bridge.[11]

In 1642 the castle was garrisoned for the king by the Earl of Cumberland and put into a state of defence, and the damaged forebuilding of Clifford's Tower was rebuilt.[12] Although the keep was frequently hit by cannon shot during the siege of 1644, it was repaired in 1652 and continued to be garrisoned and kept in repair until 23 April 1684 when it was gutted by fire.

In 1667–8 the Grand Jury House on the site of the present Assize Courts was rebuilt, or perhaps, as views suggest, only refronted, costing the North Riding £133 6*s.* 8*d.*, and in 1670 the Crown End of the Common Hall was repaired.[13] Since in 1674 the Common Hall, on part of the site of the existing Female Prison, was rebuilt at a cost of £650 the previous repairs were presumably to a dilapidated mediaeval building.[14] Building work continued, for in 1678–9 the walls flanking the approach were repaired, and in 1684–5 the *Nisi prius* side of the castle, presumably in the new hall, was made more capacious.[15] The prison accommodation had for long been inadequate: the keeper petitioned the Privy Council on its ruinous condition in 1636,[16] and in 1653 warders complained that prisoners had broken through the weak walls of the low gaol and escaped. Pursuit was hindered by the retention of the keys of the 'back gates' by the garrison in Clifford's Tower.[17] The next work contemplated by the county magistrates was a spacious and impressive prison.

The appearance of the mediaeval castle at the end of the 17th century can be reconstructed from Archer's plan of *c.* 1682 (in York City Library) and by various drawings, notably those by Francis Place of *c.* 1700 (Pls. 2, 3, 60)[18]. On the S. an earth dam held up the waters of the Foss to form the King's Fishpond, stretching for ½ mile to Monk Bridge and some 400 ft. wide at the dam. At the W. end of the dam were the Castle Mills. From the dam a stone bridge terminating in a drawbridge had formerly led to the S. gatehouse which had a lofty pointed archway between two drum towers, but which was blocked and disused by 1682. The gate to the N., also flanked by semicircular towers, and with a pointed archway of several orders, was approached by another stone bridge continuing the line of Castlegate. On the curving E. curtain wall between the two gates there were four semicircular towers; at the S. angle there was a round tower. Another tower at the W. angle had disappeared, probably by the time of Leland and certainly by 1682. A gate in the N.W. wall led to a stone bridge across the moat surrounding the motte.

Within the bailey had stood a great hall, a lesser hall with a chapel adjoining it, which were probably the Courthouse and Chapel shown against the E. wall on Archer's plan, kitchens, a gaol and a mint. A well E.

---

[1] PRO E101/501/8; Salzman, 304.
[2] PRO E101/501/11.
[3] H. Jenkinson and C. Johnson, *English Court Hand* (1915), 180–4, pl. XXIIIB.
[4] Bod. Lib. MS Dodsworth 157, *c.* 1619.
[5] BM, Harl. MS 433, f. 183v, 187; *YCR*, II, 9–10.
[6] *CLP: For. and Dom.* Henry VIII, vii, 167.
[7] Hist. MSS Com. *Calendar of the Shrewsbury and Talbot Papers*, I, 80th Report, pt. I (1966). 27,
[8] Hist. MSS Com. *MSS Var. Coll.*, II, 55th Report (1903), 348; NR Rec. Soc., III, 4.
[9] M. Claridge, *Margaret Clitherow* (1966), 71–2.
[10] *CSP: Dom. 1595–7*, 261; B31, ff. 191v, 192, 199v–201, 218v–20, 314v–15v.
[11] NR Rec. Soc., III, 43.
[12] Torr, 105; Drake, 289.
[13] NR Rec. Soc., VI, 144.
[14] *ibid.*, 187; Cooper (1911), 211.
[15] NR Rec. Soc., VII, 21, 76.
[16] *CSP: Dom. 1636*, 307.
[17] Surtees Soc., XL, xxxiv.
[18] P.S. *see* p. 176.

of the 17th-century Grand Jury House was no doubt mediaeval. Outside the southern extremity of the bailey, outside the main wall and at the edge of the moat was a low wall, apparently the 'flanker' partly demolished in 1596, with a rounded tower and an outer gate adjoining it; the gate had led towards St. George's Chapel. A stump of wall shown by Archer to the E. of the N. gate may also have cut off access to the banks below the curtain wall.

Lightly indicated on Archer's plan are the outlines of six bastions at intervals around the bailey wall. These are either his own suggestions for modernising the defences of the castle or perhaps the remains of works mentioned by Evelyn in 1654.[1] Another feature outside the walls of which there is now no trace is 'Sir Harry Slingsby's Walk', recorded by Drake.[2]

The appearance of the two buildings replaced in the 18th century by the Female Prison and Assize Courts is known from contemporary views.[3] The Moot Hall or Sessions House on the E. of the bailey was single-storeyed, of brick with stone dressings and with a hipped roof. In plan it was a rectangle with two porches projecting from the W. side near the ends. The elevations were divided into bays by pilasters.

The Grand Jury House opposite on the S.W. was apparently adapted from a mediaeval building, judging by the two tall chimneystacks and irregular windows on the W. side. It also was rectangular, but of two storeys, of brick with stone dressings towards the castle yard, and with a hipped roof. The façade with rusticated angles and a low plinth was divided into three bays by pilasters; the windows of the ground floor had rounded pediments and the doorway had a rusticated surround with key block below a triangular pediment. A low annexe had lain to the N.W. and the old well remained in front, at first with an ornamental head and later fitted with a pump.

The centre of the bailey or castle yard has long been grassed. It was levelled in 1777 when gravel paths were also made.[4] Since about 1790 it has had at its centre a round or oval lawn, popularly known as the 'Eye of the Ridings'. County elections for the whole of Yorkshire were held here until 1831 and elections for the North Riding until 1882. Proclamations of the accession of monarchs and of the declaration of war or peace were also made in the bailey. When the castle became a regular place of execution in 1802, replacing the York Tyburn on the Knavesmire, criminals were hanged on the New Drop in the angle between the Assize Courts and the bailey wall. A design for its mechanism survives.[5] Its use was discontinued in 1868, and until 1896 executions took place inside the prison walls at the N. end of the Female Prison.

In 1701–5 the new County Gaol (now known as the Debtors' Prison) was built on the S. side of the bailey, perhaps to the designs of William Wakefield, and in the following decades the castle was altered by the removal of some towers (1708), the draining of the wet ditch on the W. (1731),[6] the demolition of the great S. gate, blocked since the Civil War[7] and the rebuilding of the N. gate (1735). A coach house for the High Sheriff was built in the castle in 1732.[8] In 1773–7 the new Assize Courts by Carr were built on the W. of the bailey, replacing the Grand Jury House. In 1780 the Female Prison designed by local builders replaced the old Moot Hall on the E. of the bailey and was enlarged in 1803. In 1805–6 a new outer wall was built to the W. on the site of a mediaeval wall.

By 1818 the prison was in urgent need of improvement and extension as pamphlets by J. J. Gurney and Sydney Smith show.[9] The provisions of the Gaol Act of 1823 also required alterations. Accordingly in 1824 the Court of Gaol Sessions resolved to enlarge the prison. Three designs exist, prepared in that year, two by Peter Atkinson and R. H. Sharp and one by Robert Wallace (Figs. pp. 62–3).[10] One Atkinson and Sharp plan was to retain the gatehouse, extend the Assize Courts and Debtors' Prison, but to demolish the Female Prison and use that site together with most of the Castle Yard for prison buildings. The other plan envisaged the demolition of the gatehouse, Female Prison, and Assize Courts, the replacement of the Female Prison by a new Courthouse, prison buildings similar to those in the first scheme on the site of the Assize Courts, and the extension of the Debtors' Prison. Wallace's design in Romanesque style retained all the existing buildings. Clifford's Tower would be altered to form a chapel above turnkeys' rooms and a kitchen in a basement on

[1] E. S. de Beer (ed.), *Diary of John Evelyn* (1955), III, 130: 'the Castle which was modernly fortified with a *Palizad* and bastions'. *See* p. 176.

[2] Drake, 286.

[3] Drake, pl. between pp. 286–7; E. Croft-Murray and P. Hilton, *Catalogue of British Drawings*, I (1960), pl. 249.

[4] *York Chronicle*, 14 March 1777.

[5] Brierley Drawings.

[6] Minster Library, Beckwith MS.

[7] Drake, 287.

[8] NR Rec. Soc., VIII, 193.

[9] J. J. Gurney, *Notes on a Visit made to some of the Prisons in Scotland and the North of England* (1819); S. Smith, *A Letter to the Committee of Magistrates of the County of York* (1824).

[10] Brierley, Leckenby, and Keighley drawings, and Castle Museum.

the site of the motte, which was to be removed. An arcaded gallery and machicolated parapet with turret would have transformed the appearance of the Tower. Seven corridors would have led from it to large prison blocks on three sides within an outer wall incorporating S. W. Waud's house, as a governor's residence, and Castlegate Postern.

The design finally adopted by the Building Committee of County Magistrates in 1825 was by P. F. Robinson and G. T. Andrews in the Tudor Gothic style. It entailed the demolition not only of the old gatehouse and of Castlegate Postern, acquired from York Corporation, but of Waud's house, bought together with the grounds around Clifford's Tower, as well as houses on the E. side of Castlegate. The total cost of the new building was £194,428 including £18,553 for the purchase of houses and extra land. The foundation stone was laid on 20 March 1826 by the High Sheriff and work went on until 1835. All buildings were in gritstone. The contractors were Hiram Craven and Sons.

A new battlemented outer wall 35 ft. high included in the prison grounds not only Clifford's Tower and the site of its moat but also a stretch of Castlegate. Entrance was by a gateway to the N.W. of the motte flanked by two drum towers. This new gatehouse, vaulted as a precaution against fire, included record rooms, offices, and a court room; fragments of its façade and interior woodwork survive (Pls. 4, 15; *below* p. 86). To the E. of the motte was a round tower for the governor's house and four radiating prison blocks within a semicircular inner enclosure. The motte was cut back at the base and retained by a wall 20 ft. high with access on the S.W. The level of the N. part of the bailey was lowered by about 5 ft. and low terraces were built along the main façades of the Assize Courts and the Female Prison. Meanwhile Clifford Street had been formed in 1881 cutting through the site of the Franciscan Friary and across the narrow Water Lanes between Castlegate and the Ouse to join Tower Street (Castlegate Postern Lane widened and re-aligned) W. of the new outer wall.

In 1900 the castle ceased to be a civil prison but became instead a military prison and so continued until the end of September 1929. In 1934 the prison buildings were sold to the City of York for £8,000. Between August and November 1935 the outer wall, gatehouse, and all the buildings later than 1824 were demolished. New municipal offices for the city were begun in 1938 N. of the motte but never completed beyond the basements. Clifford's Tower is now (1980) in the care of the Department of the Environment, the two prison blocks house the Castle Museum, and the Assize Courts still serve their original purpose. In 1969 a gallery was built to link the museum in the Female Prison with that in the Debtors' Prison.[1]

In illustrating the following account, the ground-floor plan and elevations of Clifford's Tower are based upon drawings prepared in the former Office of Works and the first-floor plan and section upon drawings by J. Ridsdale Tate; the plans and elevations of the 18th-century court and prison buildings are based upon drawings by Mr. Kenneth Ward.

CLIFFORD'S TOWER (Pls. 1–8; Figs. pp. 68–72) is a quadrilobate stone tower, originally of two storeys, now a roofless shell. It was built in 1245–62 by order of Henry III and probably to the design of Henry de Reyns. The plan is similar to that of keeps at Ambléný (Aisne) and Étampes (Essonne) in France and of the larger and once loftier keep at Pontefract. The origin of its present name, first recorded in 1596, is uncertain but perhaps connected with the claim of the Clifford family to be hereditary constables. In mediaeval documents it was normally described as 'the great tower'. References to payments for its construction between 1244 and 1312 have been collected.[2]

In 1298 it was prepared to house the Treasury of the Receipt of the Exchequer, again installed there in 1322 and 1361–2.[3] In 1312 the sheriff was ordered to cover with lead the chapel in the tower which had been reconstructed and to complete a palisade and ditch near the castle.[4] Extensive floods in 1315–16 softened the soil of the motte, necessitating repairs.[5] Repairs to the tower were also ordered in 1360,[6] and twelve loads of lead were to be bought to cover the houses within the tower.[7] In 1325 it was reported that the lead on the great tower was mostly consumed and that the bridge from the tower to the castle and the breastwork around it needed repair.[8] Repairs to the keep may have been

---

[1] *See also King's Works* (1963), I, 116, II, 889–94; Cooper (1911); Drake, 286–8; Hargrove, II, 225–59; King, 259–60; O'Neill (1934, 1936, 1939); Pressly (1950); RCHM, *York City*, I, 68–9; Sheahan and Whellan, I, 337–43, 601–4; Salzman, *passim*; Twyford and Griffiths, (1880); VCH, *York*, 521–8; Renn (1971).

[2] *Arch. J.*, CXI (1954), 153–9.

[3] PRO Exchequer KR E159/71/41d; *CCR, 1327–30*, 162; Various Accounts E101/598/6.

[4] *CCR, 1307–13*. 424.

[5] *CIM*, II, no. 244; *CCR, 1313–18*, 262.

[6] *CCR, 1318–23*, 189.

[7] *CCR, 1323–7*, 14.

[8] *CCR, 1323–7*, 299

made in 1327 if it is identifiable as the tower 'within the castle' on which Henry of Lincoln, a carpenter, spent £28 13*s.* 9*d.* on renewing the lead roof, repairing the walls, and plastering a room over the entrance as a residence for the Queen mother Isabella.[1] In 1334 repairs to the palisades around the tower were again ordered, and at about the same time are mentioned the 'wooden walls of the high tower', possibly 'the hoardings called Le bretesse within the tower' and around the parapet.[2]

The tower was handed over to the Countess of Buchan in 1338 for her use while her husband was on service abroad with the king.[3] An inquisition made in January 1360 revealed that the tower was split from top to bottom in two places, being defects which had started over 40 years before, that loss of lead had caused damage to the roof, that locks, staples, and bars were missing from the doors, and that the wooden breastwork ('bretagium') around the tower had not only lost its gate but had gradually decayed during the past two decades.[4] In the next five years some £800 was spent on repairs to the great tower and to the rest of the castle. Iron for the stays of the breastwork is mentioned in 1362.[5]

Little is known of the history of the tower for the next two centuries: like the castle, it was apparently allowed to fall into decay. When in 1478 Edward IV granted the constableship of the tower and castle to Sir Robert Ryther he stated his intention of repairing them.[6] On 12 July 1537 Robert Aske was hung in chains from the summit of the tower and a year later the head of Lancaster Herald, Thomas Miller, was set beside Aske's body.[7] At about this time, however, Leland noted that 'the arx is al in ruine'.[8]

Robert Redhead's attempt to demolish the tower in 1596 was only stopped by vigorous protests from the city council which sent petitions to the Lord Chancellor, the Lord Treasurer, and the Earl of Cumberland.[9] One petition complained that they would have no 'other buildinge for showe of this cittye sarve of but onlye the minster and churche steples if the said towre shold be pulled downe'. Another described it 'as standing a great height, and upon a very rare mount, it is an exceeding ornament to the city'. It was suggested that it could be restored either as a gaol or a record office for the city. A committee set up by the Archbishop recommended against its destruction.[10] When Redhead renewed his demolition of the upper part in 1597 piles of stones are mentioned 'which had been pulled downe of the inside of the buildings of the said towre', perhaps after removal of the roof.[11] The citizens urged that if the government was set on its destruction they should have the stone for repairing the walls and Ouse Bridge. However, the protests were successful and Redhead desisted.

In 1614 James I granted Clifford's Tower and its motte to Edmund Duffield and Henry Babington, who conveyed it to Francis Darley in 1616.[12] In 1642, however, the castle was garrisoned for the king by the Earl of Cumberland, who regarded himself as its hereditary captain.[13] In January 1643 the number of the garrison was 200 under Col. Sir John Cobb. At this time the forebuilding was restored, new floors and roof were added, including a wooden platform on the roof on which two demi-culverins and a saker were mounted. Fire from one of these guns effectively delayed the movement of a heavy gun to the Parliamentary battery on Lamel Hill.[14] The besiegers, however, claimed that a breach was made in the tower.[15] After the surrender of York in 1644 the tower still held a garrison. An order of the House of Commons made on 26 February 1645/6 stated that this should consist of 60 infantry. Its commanders were Capt. Thomas Dickenson in 1651, Lieut. John Fugill in 1657, and Lieut. Gervase Harestaffe in 1659. Cromwell was greeted by a salute of guns from the tower when he passed through York in 1650.[16] John Rogers, mayor of Hull, spent £600 on repairs to it and the defences of Hull in 1652.[17] Lt. Col. Edward Salmon petitioned for repayment of £622 spent on work there and at Hull.[18] Cannon and 3,000 muskets from the tower and castle were transferred to Hull and London in 1650 and 1652.[19] After the Restoration stores of arms there were inspected and retained.[20] Sir Henry Cholmeley petitioned Charles II for compensation for his loss of the tower which he had intended to pull down.[21] In 1662 Major Scott successfully petitioned the king for the post of Commander of 'Clifford's Castle' with a command of 40 men since he had been the governor of the disbanded garrison and

1 Pipe Roll, E372/173 rot. 42d.
2 E598/6; *CCR, 1333–7*, 284.
3 *CCR, 1337–9*, 322.
4 *CIM*, III, *1348–77*, 130–2 no. 366.
5 PRO, E101/598/6.
6 *CPR. 1476–85*, 127.
7 *CSP, Henry VIII 1537*, II, 87, 96.
8 *see* p.21.
9 B31, ff. 191v, 192, 199v–201, 218v–220.
10 *CSP: Dom. 1595–7*. 26.
11 B31, ff. 314v–15v.
12 Cooper (1911), 168–9.
13 Slingsby, *Diary*, 82.
14 Torr, 109.
15 *Hulls Managing of the Kingdoms Cause* (1644), 27.
16 Drake, 172.
17 *CSP: Dom. 1651–2*, 619; *Cal. Treasury Bks. 1660–7*, 525.
18 *CSP: Dom. 1653–E*, 331.
19 *CSP: Dom. 1650*, 276; *1650–1*, 175.
20 *CSP: Dom. 1661–2*, 132.
21 *CSP: Dom. 1660–1*, 446.

**

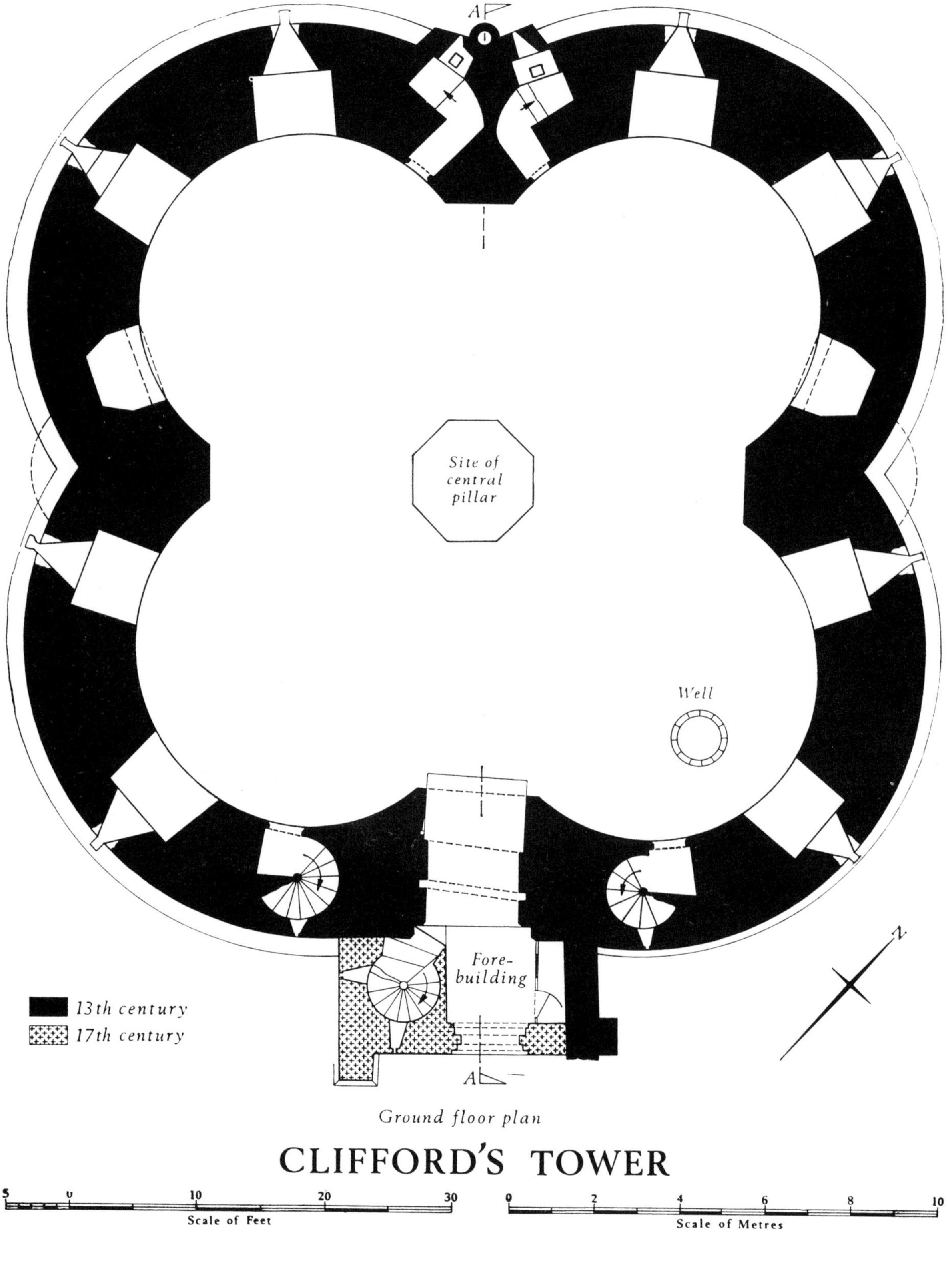

A
Site of central pillar
Well
Fore-building
13th century
17th century
A
N
Ground floor plan
CLIFFORD'S TOWER
5 0 10 20 30
Scale of Feet
0 2 4 6 8 10
Scale of Metres

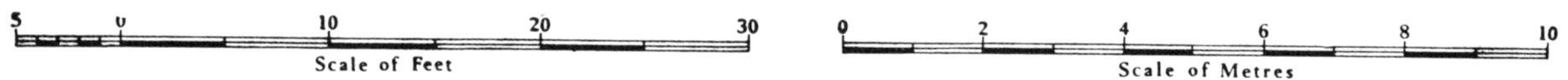

First floor plan

CLIFFORD'S TOWER

CLIFFORD'S TOWER

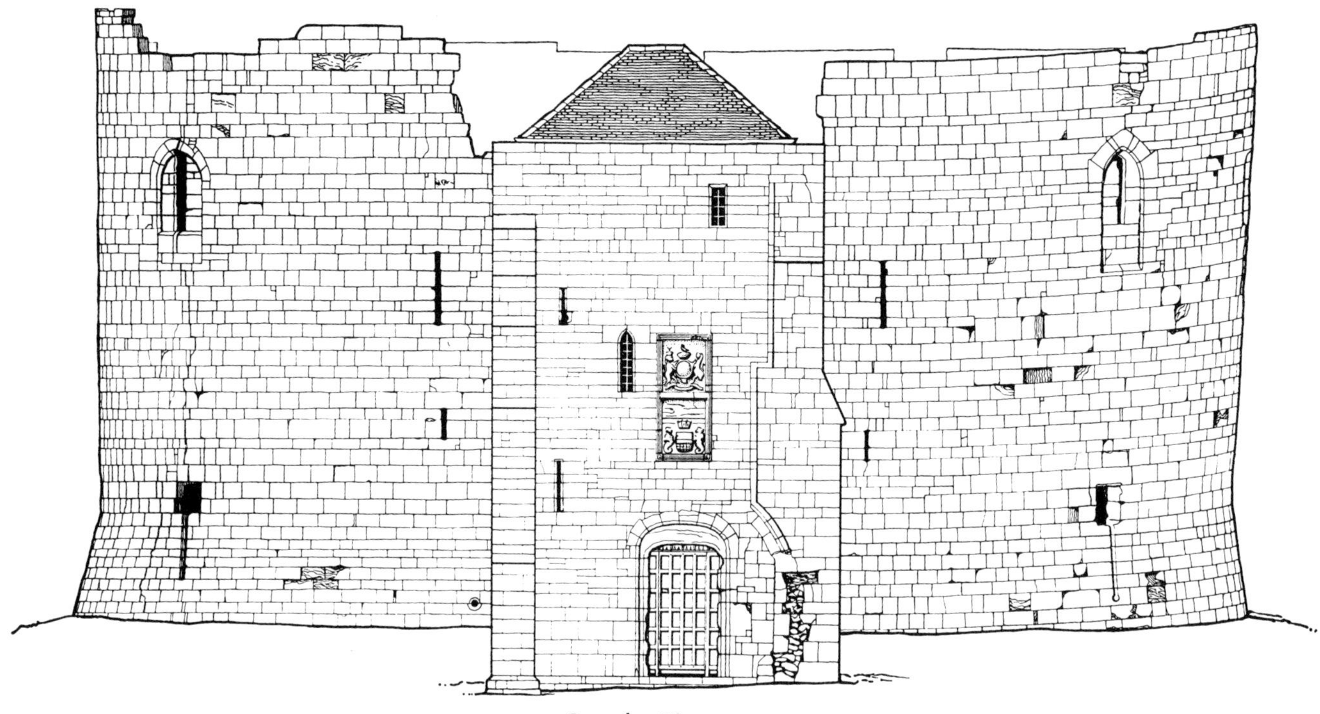

South Elevation

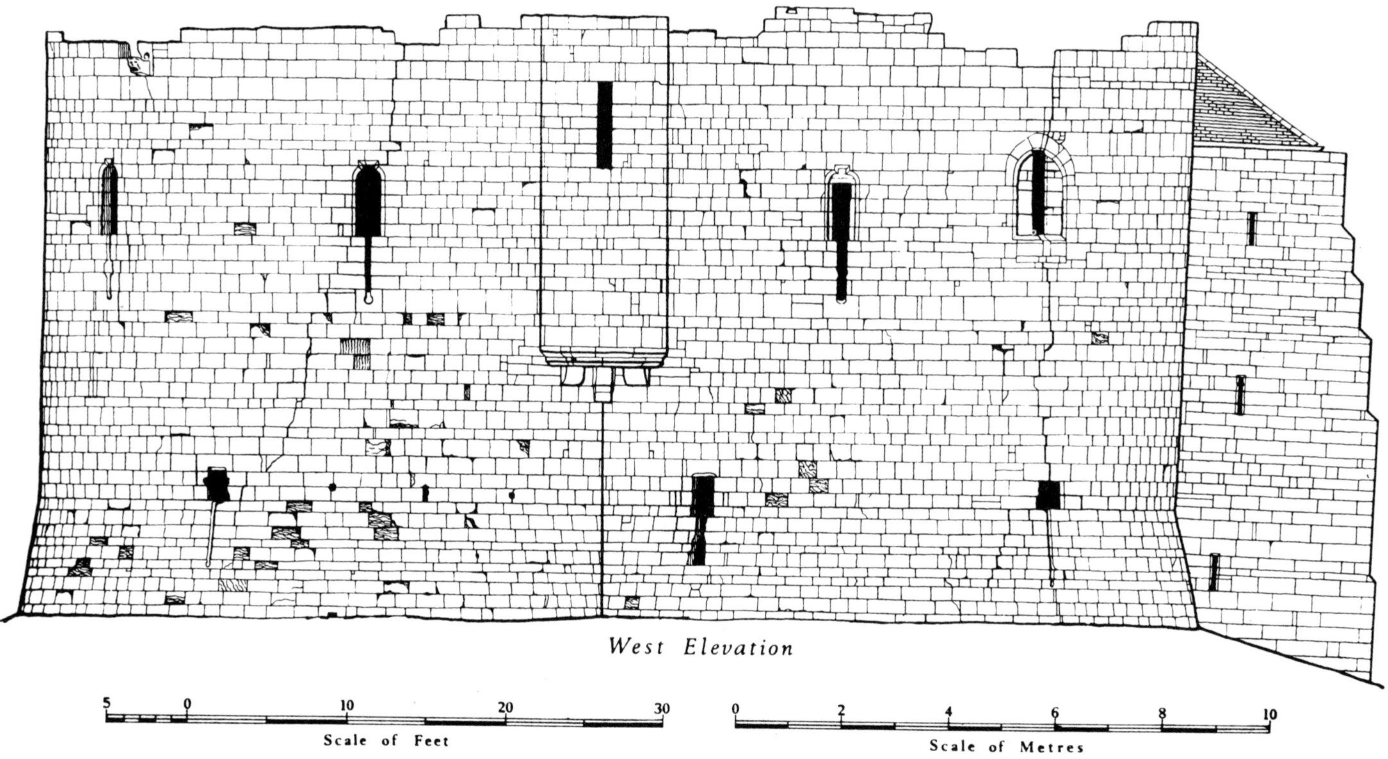

West Elevation

CLIFFORD'S TOWER

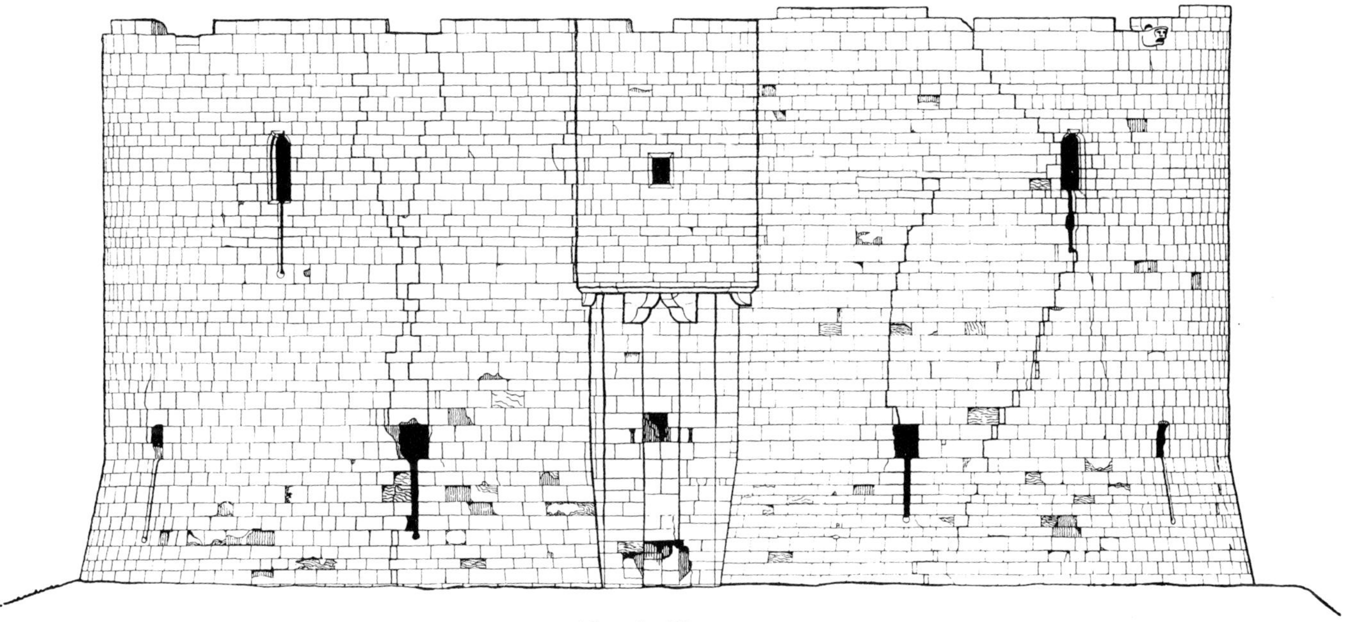

North Elevation

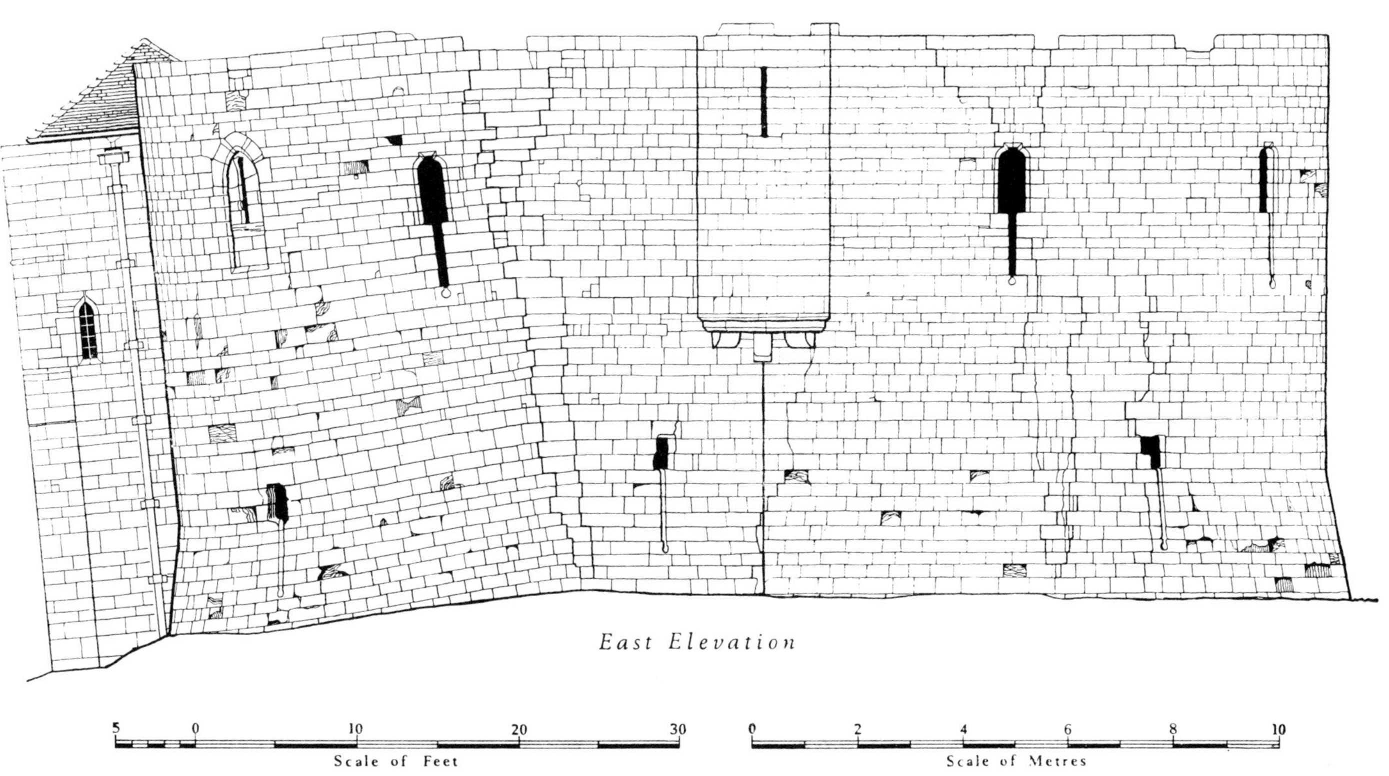

East Elevation

5 0 10 20 30

Scale of Feet

0 2 4 6 8 10

Scale of Metres

***

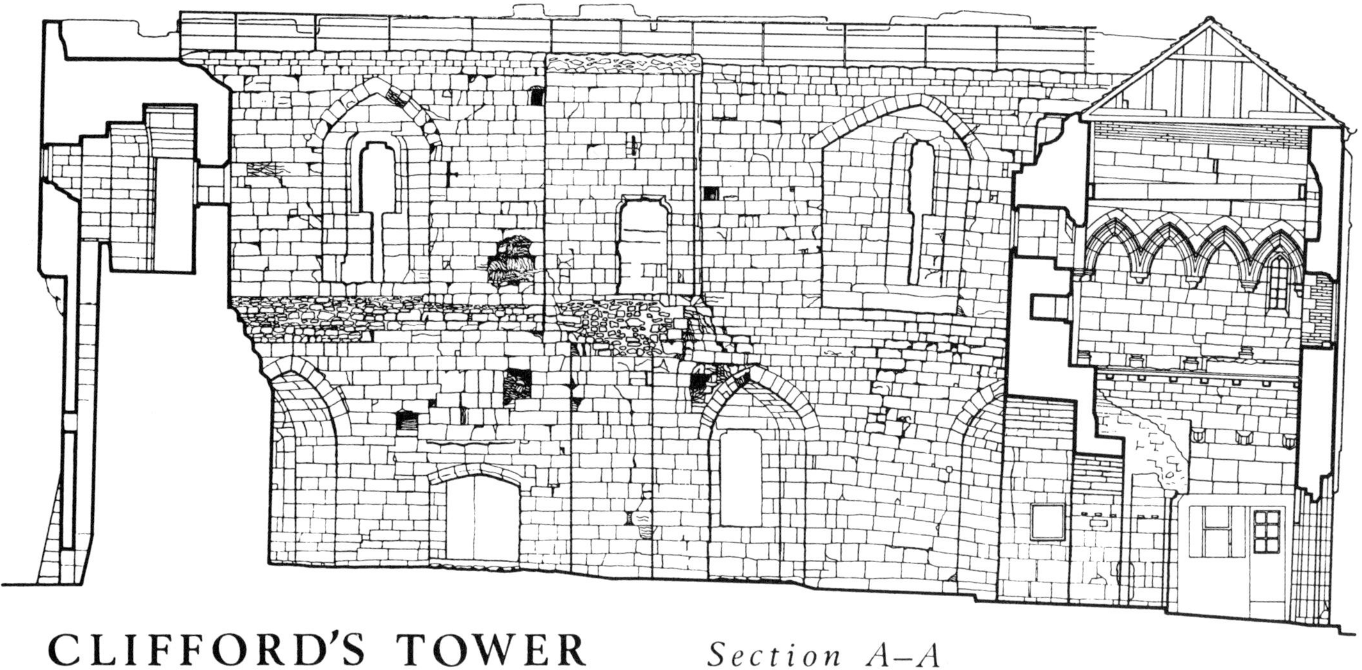

CLIFFORD'S TOWER *Section A–A*

5 0 10 20 30 Feet 0 5 10 Metres

it was to be used as a magazine.[1] Its capture was an alleged aim of plots in 1662 and 1663.[2] George Fox was imprisoned in a great chamber, apparently in the tower, in 1665.[3] When Keep wrote in 1680 the tower was 'sufficiently strong haveing some cannon, two culverins, and a sacker or two on the platforme, with a continuall garrison therein for its defence'.[4]

When Sir John Reresby took possession of the tower as Governor of York on 27 June 1682 he found it 'in pretty good condition as to repairs and stoors (pouder only excepted and cannon)'.[5] In October of that year, when Sir Christopher Musgrave, Lieutenant of the Ordnance, inspected the castle and 'tooke the dimension and scituation of the Tower and Castle by the helpe of a surveyer brought with him to that purpas' (probably James Archer), he told Reresby that the king 'would be at the charge to repair the defects of the Tower (especially the parapet which was too weake), and to bring the river about it'.[6] In April 1682 Thoresby saw there arms for about 3,000 men and a large crocodile.[7]

On 23 April 1684, however, after a salute of seven guns had been fired from it in honour of St. George's Day, 'the Tower was sett on fire and all the inside of it burnt; only the powder and some part of the arms were saved'.[8] This fire was popularly supposed to be deliberate, since toasts had been drunk in the city 'to the demolition of the Minced Pie', as the tower was derisively called. In spite of the gutting of the building, powder was still stored there until 1690 and a guard maintained at the entrance.[9] Salutes were also still fired from it by the three or four cannon saved from the fire, as in February 1687/8 when the gunner accidentally blew himself into the moat, and in October 1688.[10] When Lord Danby and others seized York for the Prince of Orange on 22 November of that year they found only three barrels of powder and some old rusty arms in the magazine.[11]

After the abandonment of Clifford's Tower as a garrison it came into private hands, passing from Lady Suzanna Thompson in 1699 to the Sowray family and

[1] *CSP: Dom. 1661–2*, 628.
[2] *CSP: Dom. 1663–4*, 234, 571.
[3] N. Penney (ed.), *George Fox, the Journal* (1911), II, 94.
[4] H. Keep, 'Monumenta Eboracensia', Trin. Coll. Camb. MS O.4.33, 107.
[5] A. Browning (ed.), *Memoirs of Sir John Reresby* (1936), 268.
[6] *ibid.*, 279–80. *See below* pp. 176–9.
[7] J. Hunter (ed.), *The Diary of Ralph Thoresby* (1830), I, 117.
[8] Browning, *op. cit.*, 336–7; Hammond MS in York City Library quoted by Cooper (1911), 183.
[9] Browning, *op. cit.*, 446; B39, ff. 16, 18.
[10] *ibid.*, 486, 519.
[11] Hist. MSS Com., *7th Rep.*, I (1879), 420.

then from 1727 to three successive generations of Samuel Wauds.[1] The motte and tower were treated as an ornamental feature in the grounds of their house to the N.E., and winding paths were made around the mound. In 1825 the house and grounds including the ruined tower were bought by the County Committee for £8,800. Demolition was at first contemplated but a pamphlet was written against this idea; other plans envisaged use as a chapel; eventually only the base of the motte was cut back and a new retaining wall built. The tower was restored in 1902 by Basil Mott at a cost of £3,000, when the S. side was underpinned. In 1915 it was placed under the guardianship of the Commissioners of H.M. Works and extensively repaired in 1920–3. In 1936 the retaining wall was partly demolished, the motte restored to its earlier shape, and a new flight of steps added.

Architectural Description. (*Note.* Although the main axis of the tower is N.N.E.–S.S.W. it is described as if the three bartizans and forebuilding faced the cardinal points.) The wall of rubble faced with finely jointed ashlar of magnesian limestone is 10 ft. thick at the base, which is battered to a height of 10 ft., and 9 ft. thick above the batter. There are several serious cracks in the masonry; the two most extensive, in the S. lobes, are probably those noted in 1360. The side of the tower is leaning 2 ft to 3 ft. to the S., but further subsidence has been arrested by work carried out since 1902.

The main tower is entered on the S. by a rectangular forebuilding restored in 1642 and later (Pl. 8). Of the stepped buttresses the eastern is 13th-century and the western 17th-century work. The S. and W. sides in mauve-tinted stone are 17th-century. On the outer face above the entrance are two square panels within a moulded frame, the upper with an achievement of the royal arms of Charles I with the royal cypher CR and the lower with the achievement of Henry Clifford, 5th Earl of Cumberland, in low relief. To the E. of the arch are the remains of the label of the 13th-century arch. A spiral staircase in the W. wall of this forebuilding leading to its upper storeys is a 17th-century addition. There is a stone bench along the inside of the E. wall of the ground floor. The tower proper is entered by a pointed archway with a portcullis slot and provision for a second pair of doors folding back to a rebate in the walls. There is a high rear arch in the wall facing the interior of the tower.

The lower floor of the main tower was probably divided into four rooms corresponding to the four lobes, and was originally covered with a wooden ceiling supported on a central octagonal pillar, of which the foundation, discovered by excavation, is now marked on the grassed interior. Each of the lobes was lit by two slits. Each slit is set in a shoulder-arched recess and ends in a circular oillet below; the rectangular enlargement of the upper part of each slit was made in *c.* 1300 perhaps when the Exchequer was housed in the castle. Signs in the sides of the recesses show that at a later date they were closed off from the main rooms by partitions. The two N. rooms each had a fireplace with a segmental arched head and a vestigial hood, and a garderobe; the two garderobes adjoined each other in the angle between the lobes and were entered through doorways with shouldered heads. The S. rooms each had a spiral staircase to the first floor entered by a shoulder-headed doorway flanking the main entrance. In addition there is a stone-lined well at least 46 ft. deep in the S.E. lobe. There is now no sign of the subdividing walls existing in 1700, which were probably of the 17th century, but beam holes, partly blocked with brick, suggest that the Civil War alterations involved the insertion of an additional floor 5 ft. below the mediaeval floor (Pls. 6, 7).

The chapel (Pl. 4), usable by 1245, occupied the first floor of the forebuilding with its floor level 3 ft. below that of the first floor of the rest of the tower. On the inside of the E. and N. walls are arcades each of four pointed arches supported on capitals with nail-head ornament; the detached shafts have gone and the bases are much damaged. Dog-tooth ornament appears in the central order of the arches. A single wider arch of this arcade returns on the W. wall above the doorway. In 1829 the arcading was partly concealed by brick pigeon-holes. The chapel is now lit by an original single lancet in the E. wall, and in the N. wall is a rectangular recess with an opening above it. Presumably there were formerly single lancets in the E. and W. walls and the altar and piscina were on the E. The windows in the S. wall are 17th-century, so too is the brickwork of the head of the spiral stair in the S.W. angle. Detached stones preserved in the chapel include a mediaeval corbel in the form of a queen's head.

The first storey of the main tower was probably once arranged in four rooms. The rooms in the N.W. and N.E. lobes were lit by two arrow slits with shoulder-arched heads. In each of the other two lobes is a larger window with a pointed head as well as an arrow slit.

[1] Cooper (1911), 180–1, 185–8, 318–30.

These windows are arranged so that only two are immediately above those of the lower storey. The larger windows in the S.W. and S.E. lobes have been partly blocked since the serious cracks pass through them. Three rounded bartizans are corbelled out in the angles between the lobes: that on the N., roofed partly with flat slabs and partly with a pointed vault, contains a large garderobe lit by a rectangular window, and a cupboard; the others house spiral staircases to the roof which could thus be reached by a separate stair from each room. All four staircases communicated with the first floor by shoulder-headed doorways. Fireplaces to heat this floor may have been carried by the central pillar.

Above the chapel in the forebuilding was a low room, reached by a wall passage opening from a now blocked door, containing the portcullis windlass, the chains of which ran through the chapel ceiling and floor. It now has a hipped tiled roof at a lower level than previously. Probably the three bartizans and forebuilding once rose above the general level of the battlements of the tower. In 1818 the chapel and the garderobe bartizan were fitted up as dovecots.

The flat roof of the tower, destroyed in 1684, had a higher square or octagonal platform in the centre around chimneys and a flag-staff. The mediaeval roof was leaded. The present parapet walk is about 2 ft. below the original level which was 35½ ft. above the ground. The merlons and tops of the bartizans and forebuilding were presumably largely removed by Redhead in the 16th century, but remains of embrasures and arrow slits in the merlons may still be seen. A view of *c.* 1700 (Pl. 7) shows wide merlons and narrow embrasures, perhaps 17th-century alterations. A waterspout with a grotesque face projects on the W.

The Motte (Pl. 2; Figs. p. 63) rises 48 ft. above the present ground level and is 220 ft. to 235 ft. in diameter. In 1902 the S. part was underpinned in concrete, and after 1935 the perimeter was restored to approximately its former profile with stones from the demolished curtain and revetting walls and from St. Mary's Abbey, covered in earth, and turfed. The base of the 19th-century revetting wall, including the gateway on the S.W., still survives, though buried. The flat top is 93 ft. to 110 ft. in diameter with a terrace 7 ft. to 30 ft. wide around the base of the tower.

Excavations by S. W. Waud in 1824 simply showed that the mound was composed of earth containing many bones and covered timberwork,[1] but those of 1902 revealed that above the natural boulder clay the structure of the mound was in four layers consisting of clay and soil, including Roman pottery and disturbed burials, from the surrounding ditch and from elsewhere.[2] Under the original ground surface there was a crouched burial in a stone cist, perhaps of the Roman cemetery to the N. and E. of the motte, though the suggestion has been made that it may have been a prehistoric burial under a round barrow.[3] Traces of timberwork at 15½ ft. and 13 ft. below the summit, the lower accompanied by much charred wood, may have been remains of the wooden tower or palisades destroyed respectively in 1190 and 1228. The upper 13 ft. of the mound, formed of 'an outer crust of firmer and more clayey material . . . round the older summit and lighter material placed within this crater' is attributable to heightening in 1245. The surrounding wet ditch was at least 30 ft. wide.

The Bailey, kidney-shaped, S.E. of the motte, contained about 3 acres, measuring some 350 ft. (E.–W.) by 300 ft. within the ramparts. On the E. and S.E. it was bounded by the Foss and on the other sides by a wet ditch 50 ft. wide. The ramparts and wooden palisade were replaced in stone during the 13th century. Excavations made in 1935 to section the defences E. of the motte revealed two shallow post-holes in a bank of compact yellow sand and two pits containing confused human bones. These were interpreted as a palisade in the Norman bank, never replaced in stone, and as later burials of plague victims.[4] However, Archer's plan and 18th-century views show that there was a stone wall on this line from 1682 onwards, and it was probably mediaeval in origin.

The remains of the castle bailey defences consist of the footings of the S. gateway, two towers, and some 260 ft. of curtain wall, built largely of magnesian limestone.

The South Gate (NG 60555135. Pl. 3; Fig. p. 75) was in use as late as 1597 but had been blocked by 1660 and was mostly demolished in 1735. Some of the mediaeval references to gates and drawbridges in the castle must have applied to it but whether it is the 'great gate' (as Cooper supposed) or the 'lesser gate' is uncer-

[1] *Yorks. Gazette*, 1 May 1824; *Gents. Mag.*, 1824, 584. [2] YPSR (1902), 68 ff. [3] RCHM, *York City*, I, 69. [4] *Ant. J.*, XIX (1939), 85–90.

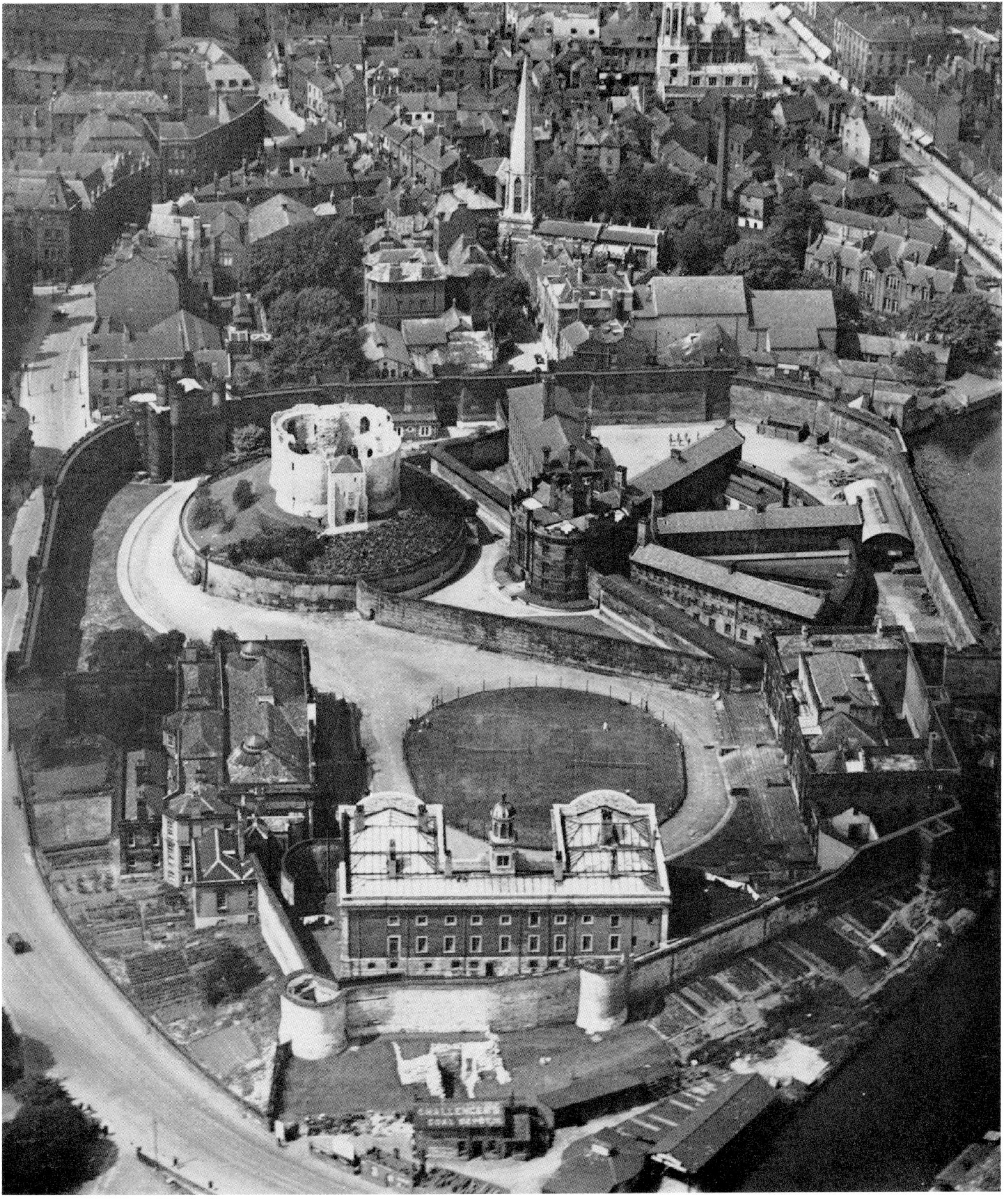

YORK CASTLE. Aerial view from S.E. in 1928. *(Aerofilms)*

CLIFFORD'S TOWER and CASTLEGATE POSTERN. Engraving by F. Place, *c.*1680.

MOTTE and CLIFFORD'S TOWER from S., 1957. 11th-century and *c.* 1250.

YORK CASTLE from S. Drawing by F. Place, 1699.

BAILEY WALLS from S., 1966. *c.* 1250 and later.

YORK CASTLE. Royal Arms (George IV) from Gatehouse. *c.* 1830.

YORK CASTLE, CLIFFORD'S TOWER. Interior of Chapel from S.E. *c.* 1250.

CLIFFORD'S TOWER. Corbels and garderobe shoots. *c.*1250.

CLIFFORD'S TOWER. Corbels of N.E. bartizan.

TOWER 23. Arrow slit and gunport. *c.* 1460.

CLIFFORD'S TOWER. Interior from S.W. *c.* 1250.

CLIFFORD'S TOWER. Interior from N.W. *c.* 1250.

CLIFFORD'S TOWER. Interior from S.W. Drawing by F. Place, *c.* 1700.

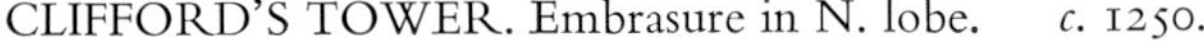

CLIFFORD'S TOWER. Embrasure in N. lobe. *c.* 1250.

SOUTH ANGLE TOWER. Embrasure. *c.* 1250.

CLIFFORD'S TOWER. Forebuilding. *c.* 1250 and 1642.

DEBTORS' PRISON. Clock turret. *c.* 1705.

ASSIZE COURTS. Section drawing by P. Atkinson, 1812.

ASSIZE COURTS. Crown Court. 1773–7; railings 1835–40.

ASSIZE COURTS. Civil Court. 1773–7 and later.

CROWN COURT. Detail of frieze. 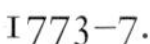 1773–7.

CIVIL COURT. Capital. 1773–7.

CROWN COURT. Detail of dome. 1773–7.

CIVIL COURT. Dome. 1773–7.

DEBTORS' PRISON. Condemned cell. 1701.

DEBTORS' PRISON. Cell door. 1701–5.

DEBTORS' PRISON. Staircase. 1701–5.

MASON'S ARMS, FISHERGATE. Fireplace from Castle Gatehouse.  *c.* 1830.

ST. HILDA'S CHURCH, TANG HALL. Cover-paten and cup from Chapel of Debtors' Prison. 1706.

DEBTORS' PRISON from N.W. 1701–5.

ASSIZE COURTS from N.E. 1773–7.

FEMALE PRISON from S.W. 1780–3 and 1802.

YORK CASTLE
South Gate

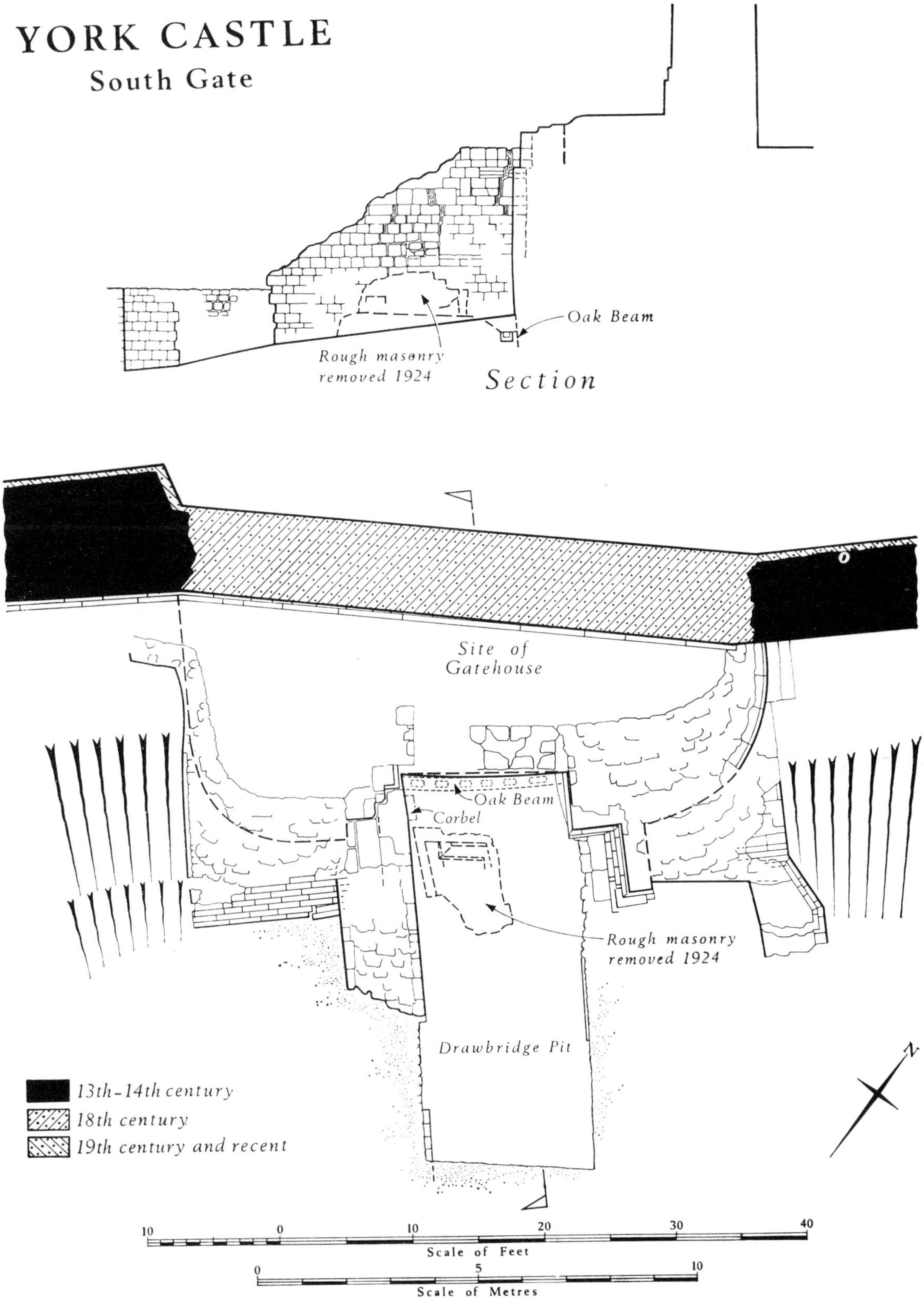

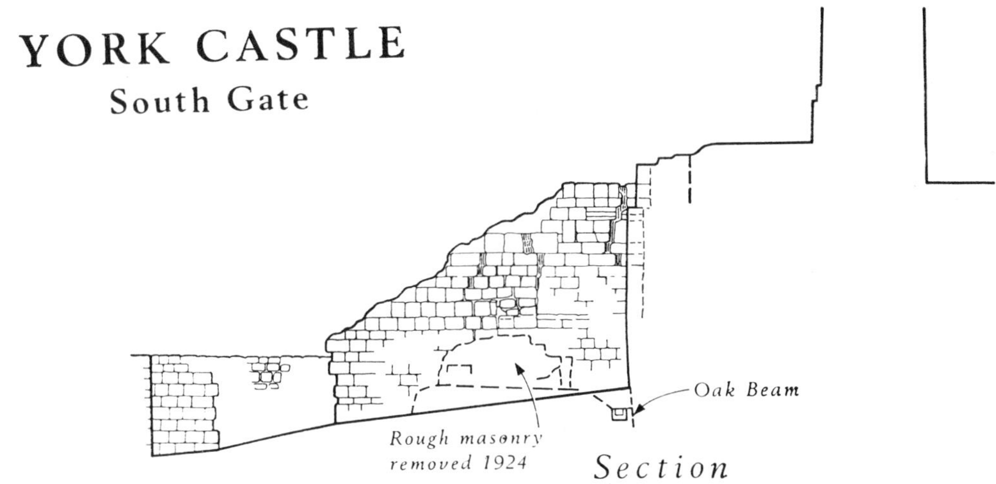

Oak Beam
Rough masonry removed 1924
Section
Site of Gatehouse
Oak Beam
Corbel
Rough masonry removed 1924
Drawbridge Pit
13th-14th century
18th century
19th century and recent
N
10 0 10 20 30 40
Scale of Feet
0 5 10
Scale of Metres

tain. The size and importance of the N.E. gate make it possible that that should rather be identified as the 'great gate'.

The footings cleared by the Office of Works in 1924 and still standing in places to a height of 11 ft. show that the passageway, 12 ft. wide, was flanked on either side by quadrant-shaped towers 16 ft. wide and projecting 16 ft. in front of the wall. Fragments of a chamfered plinth and rectangular stepped bases survive. Views drawn before its demolition (Pl. 3) show that the gate was recessed below a tall arch as at Nottingham and Tonbridge Castles and that the crenellated towers, of at least three storeys, stood some 40 ft. high. The archway had been blocked, probably in the Civil War, and a mass of masonry added externally against its lower half. From Archer's plan of *c.* 1682 it seems that the gatehouse projected about 30 ft. from inside the curtain wall.

A drawbridge pit 12 ft. deep survives in front of the site of the gate. A mass of masonry removed subsequent to excavation may have supported the drawbridge. The remains suggest that the gateway was modified in the 14th century by the addition of two buttresses to the N.E. tower and a wall on the S.W. side of the pit. In the later Middle Ages the gate was probably approached from the Castle Mills through a small pointed-arched doorway drawn by Halfpenny,[1] up a ramp running

[1] *Fragmenta Vetusta*, Pl. 9.

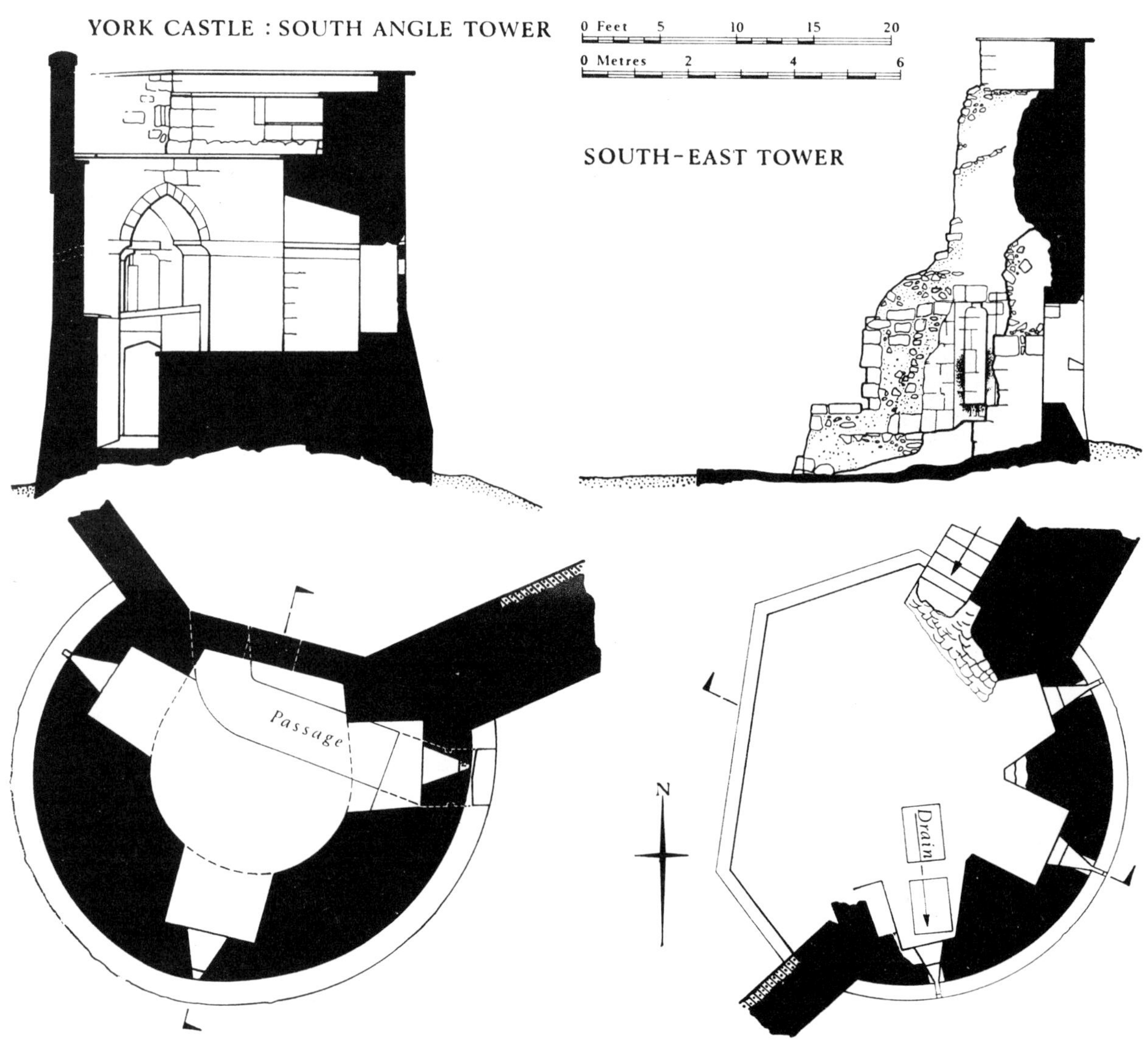

YORK CASTLE : The Bailey Wall

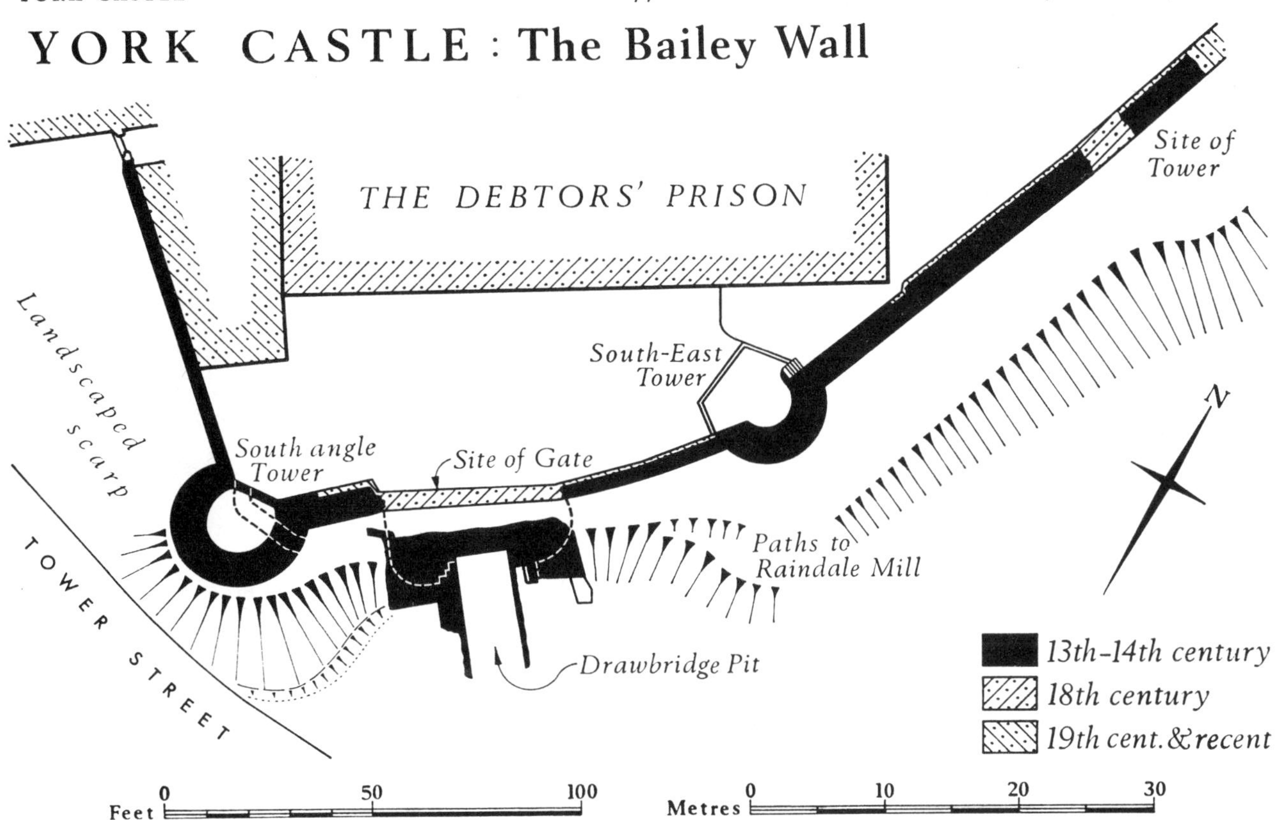

S.W.–N.E. parallel to the curtain wall and then across the drawbridge. This outer doorway was flanked on the S.W. by a rounded tower with a chamfered plinth at its base and at least one cruciform arrow slit and by a similar arrow slit in a wall to the N.W., but these remains of outer defences were destroyed in 1805 (Fig. p. 75).

The South Angle Tower (NG 60545134. Pls. 3, 7; Fig. p. 76), called in 1326 'the tower in the angle towards the mills',[1] is threequarters of a circle on plan, and the base is battered. The floor is 9 ft. above the present general ground level though in part removed in the 19th century for a passage leading from the interior of the bailey out through a doorway in the E. side of the tower. At the floor level three vertical arrow slits remain; they are under shouldered heads internally set in arched embrasures 6 ft. wide and 10 ft. high. An upper floor has been removed, and the arrow slits, housings for wooden hoardings, and crenellated parapet, visible in Place's drawings, have been replaced by a parapet walk on two levels with broad embrasures. In the N.E. side towards the bailey is a blocked shoulder-headed doorway below a wider and taller pointed arch.

The South-east Tower (NG 60575137. Pl. 3; Fig. p. 76) is semicircular and battered at the base. The original ground-floor level was 2 ft. to 3 ft. higher than at present, but fragments of the floor remain in the recesses. There are five cruciform arrow slits, arranged on two levels, under shouldered heads internally and formerly set in arched embrasures, most of which have been cut away. Two rectangular pits in the tower floor reveal a stone-lined drain, $2\frac{1}{2}$ ft. wide and $3\frac{3}{4}$ ft. deep, running N.–S. and apparently contemporary with the Debtors' Prison.

The Bailey Wall (Pls. 1, 3; Fig. above), 4 ft. to 8 ft. thick and 25 ft. high, has been much patched and in places rebuilt, thickened internally, and heightened with gritstone and brick, all in the 18th and 19th centuries. A wall walk has brick parapets to the E. stretch and is there drained by stone spouts projecting externally. Straight joints and changes in walling reveal the sites of the S. Gate and of a tower 80 ft. N.E. of the existing S.E. tower. The length of wall between the S. angle and

1 PRO Chancery, Misc. Inq. C145/102 (13.

the Assize Courts appears to be an entire 19th-century rebuilding and bears simple masons' marks. A mediaeval arched doorway in the angle of the wall and the Assize Courts was renewed at this time. Within the bailey, against the wall near the Female Prison, a series of seven identical vaulted lavatories of the early 19th century is notable for the careful finish of the masonry and the height (11¾ ft.) of the individual rooms.

THE DEBTORS' PRISON (Pls. 9, 14, 16; Figs. pp. 79, 80, 81), of two storeys and basement, has walls of magnesian limestone and brick and roofs covered with lead and slates.

The building, since 1952 part of the Castle Museum, was erected in 1701–5 as a County Gaol under the provisions of an Act of Parliament (11 William III, cap. 19). Stone from the ruinous parts of the castle and the King's Manor was granted for the purpose in 1701.[1] The architect is unknown but may have been William Wakefield of Huby; Wakefield was employed to build Duncombe Park by Thomas Duncombe, High Sheriff of Yorkshire in 1727, and was later concerned as a justice with repairs to the castle. The curved pediments on the fronts of the wings are an unusual motif, paralleled earlier in England though in more conventional form at Robert Hooke's Bethlehem Hospital, London (1674–6), and more closely, and contemporaneously, on Vanbrugh's King William Block at the Royal Hospital, Greenwich (1698–1723). The design has affinities with work by Wren and Vanbrugh, and the building is notable as an early example in the English baroque style. The accommodation as a prison was admired by Defoe and Howard but criticised by Gurney in 1819.[2] Hargrove gives a full description of the internal arrangements in 1818.[3] After the extensions to the prison in 1824–35 the building was modified and used as quarters for the warders. Details of the prison arrangements and life there as experienced by prisoners can be found in James Montgomery's poems '*Prison Amusements*', written in 1796, and in an anonymous account of *One Night spent in the Condemned Hole, York Castle, in April 1810*. The system in force after the rebuilding and extension is summarised in *Rules and Regulations for the Government of York Castle* (1843).

Architectural Description. (*Note.* The building is described as if facing due N.) The main E.–W. range has two wings projecting to the N. The N. front, the imposing principal façade, forms a symmetrical composition centred on an elaborated bay over which rises a clock turret. The main entrances were originally at first-floor level in the N. ends of the wings, approached by flights of steps, now removed, and leading into the Governor's quarters in the E. wing and the chapel in the W. wing. The area between the wings was formerly enclosed by railings to provide an exercise yard for debtors. The main entrance is now central, on the ground floor. The basement on all sides is given an appearance of strength by rusticated stone facing rising from a plinth to a bold ashlar band at first-floor level, which thus forms the podium to the colossal order above. Only the N. side is entirely faced in ashlar. Roman-Doric pilasters rise through the two main storeys to support a continuous entablature and a parapet. The coupled pilasters flanking the centre bay are rusticated and have a full Doric entablature; for the rest, the pilasters and entablature are plain. The parapet returns in shallow pedestal form above the pilasters except over the three middle bays of each of the two wings, where it provides the abutment and springing for a curved pedimental feature of impressive size. The windows generally are rectangular, with keyblocks, and fitted with timber mullioned-and-transomed, or mullioned, frames. Only the second-floor window in the central bay is round-headed since it occupies the upper part of a tall rusticated wall-arch framed between the coupled pilasters. Above the parapet over the central bay rises the clock tower and crowning cupola (Pl. 9). The tower of ashlar, has a moulded surround to the square clock face and is flanked by squat scrolls. The cupola is octagonal and with round-headed arches in each face; the dome is lead-covered and has a ball-finial and weathervane. The original clock, made in 1716 by John Terry of York, had a single hand replaced by a pair in 1854, when a new escapement was provided. A single hand has recently been restored.

Subsequent to completion of the building the returns of the pilasters in the re-entrant angles have been cut away, and in 1966 the pedimental features were dismantled and rebuilt with concrete-beam reinforcement.[4] Among prisoners' graffiti on the walls is a verse: 'This Prison is a House of Care / A Grave For Man Alive / A Touch Stone to Try A Friend / No Place For Man to Thrive / 1820'.

The S. side of the prison has ashlar facing to the

[1] *Cal. Treasury Bks. 1700–1701*, 229, 262.
[2] Quoted by Cooper (1911), 211, 220–4, 227–32.
[3] II, 232–40.
[4] *The Structural Engineer*, 46 (1968), 175–6.

THE DEBTORS' PRISON

FRONT ELEVATION

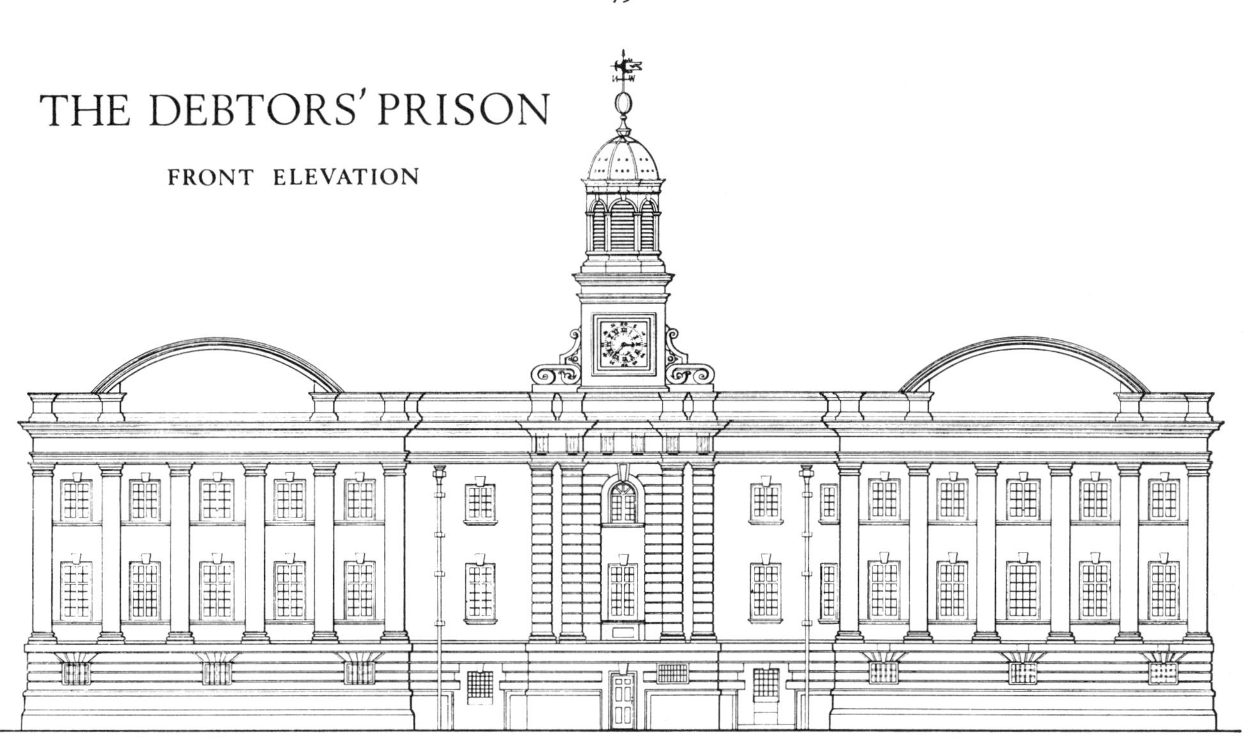

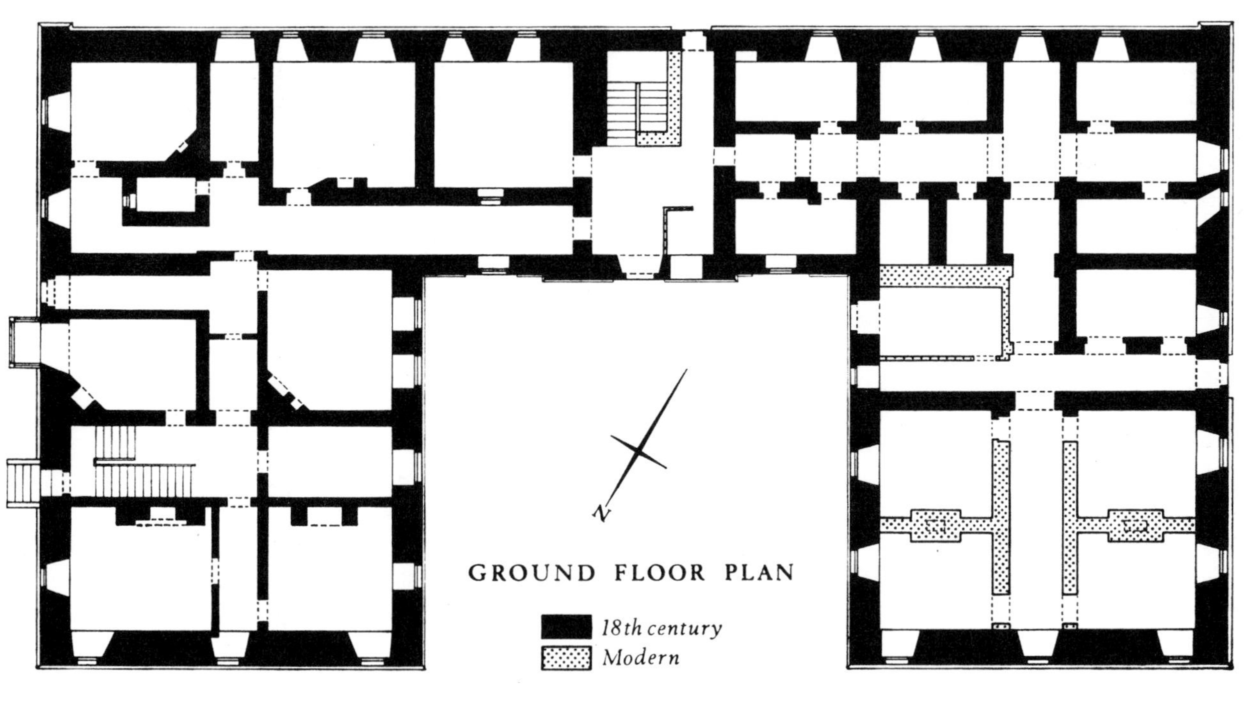

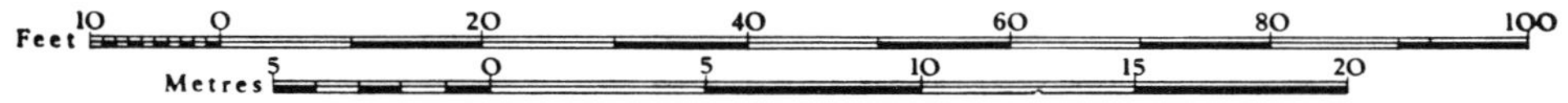

THE DEBTORS' PRISON

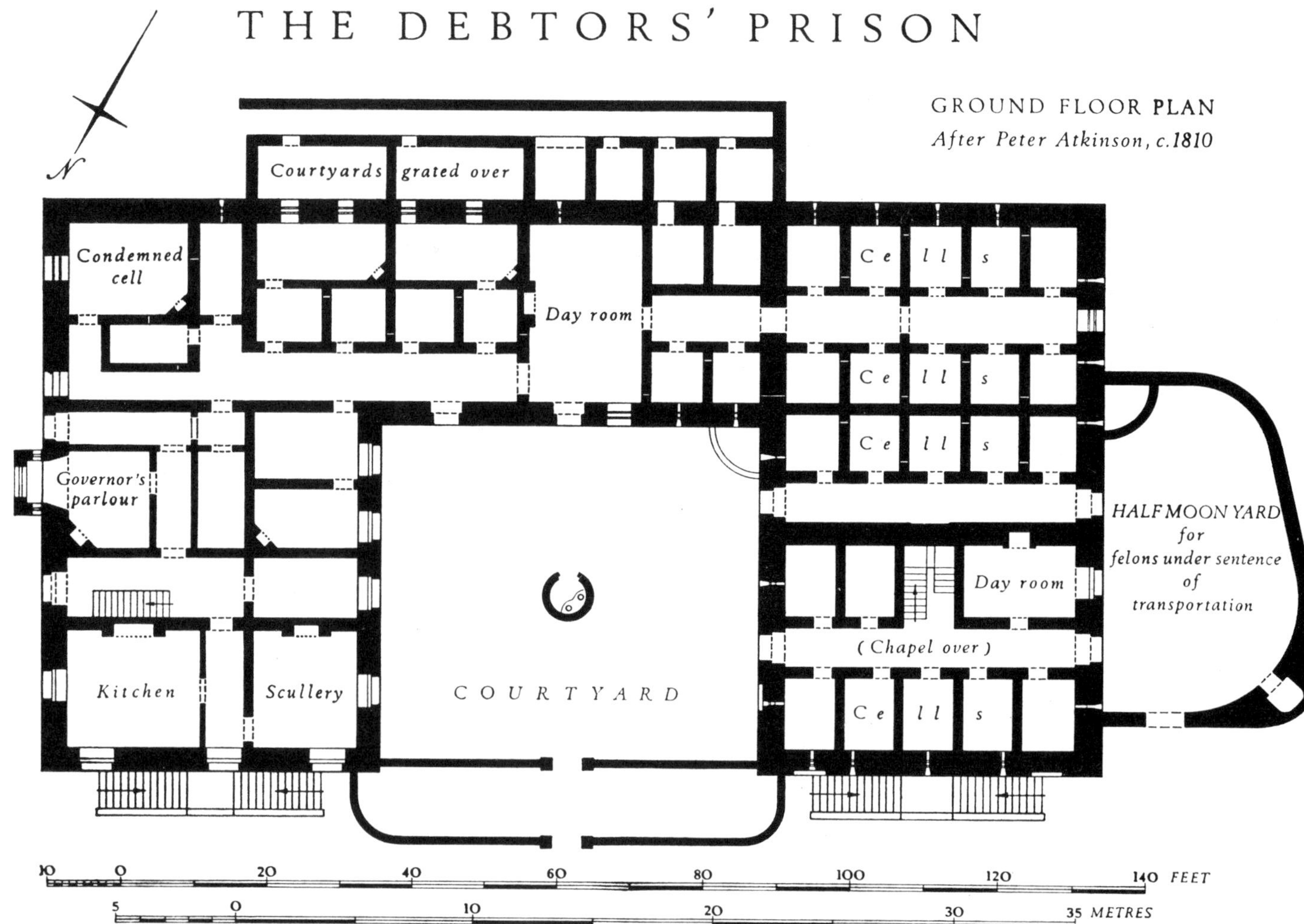

basement, but the upper storeys are brick-faced except for the pilasters at each end, the entablature, and the window dressings. The basement has a chamfered plinth and a simple band at the level of the window sills. A projecting plat band at first-floor level has been trimmed back. Dowel holes indicate the position of the iron gratings which covered the condemned prisoners' exercise yard at the E. end. The basement windows are square with heavy iron stanchions, and the nine first-floor windows have simple architraves with keyblocks to the flat arches, moulded sills, and timber casements. The entablature has a moulded cornice and plain frieze; the brick parapet above has an ashlar capping. There are original lead waterheads and down pipes, the former of inverted bell form.

The W. end elevation is similar to the S. side but the ashlar entablature is not continuous, being confined to the ends. An external stairway, now removed, once led to a doorway near the S. end at first-floor level. The Half Moon Yard or Unshackling Court adjoining this side, once used for prisoners awaiting transportation, was roofed over in 1959 to form an extension to the Museum. There are several graffiti by prisoners on either side of the doorway from the W. wing.

The E. end elevation is more elaborate than the W., with the ashlar pilasters flanking the central bay as well as at each end. A rectangular central bay window at basement level lights the former Governor's parlour. At second-floor level there is a moulded band, and below the windows, which have ashlar keyblocks and architraves, are stone aprons with sunk panels.

Inside, the ground floor has been modified to adapt

it for warders' quarters and then a museum. Pairs of adjacent cells have consequently been combined and a cross passage made in the W. wing. A new flight of stairs in the central room of the main range is now the principal approach to the upper floors. The cells have brick vaulted ceilings and many retain their iron-bound doors. The larger cell in the S.E. angle remains in its original condition (Pl. 14); like the adjacent cells to the S.W., it was used for condemned felons and was known as 'Pompey's Parlour'. There is a simple fireplace in its N.W. angle, a wrought-iron bed frame supported on stone blocks, and a stone table with a circular central hole, for a charcoal stove. The iron grilles cutting off the wings remain in the main corridors. The rooms in the N.E. wing used by the Governor's staff are now lavatories and staff rooms but the staircase remains (Pl. 14). It has a closed string with heavy turned balusters and moulded oak handrail.

There are graffiti in the cells of the W. wing, of which the most notable are a crucifix, ships, a castle, etc. On the wall at the E. end of the main corridor flagstones with prisoners' inscriptions from the Female Prison are displayed. These include a representation of a man with a dog shooting at a pheasant in a tree with the words 'Joseph Ray Aged 23, 1831' and another reading 'F. Otter aged / 37 from Licolm/ s transporte(d) for 14 years / 1829'.

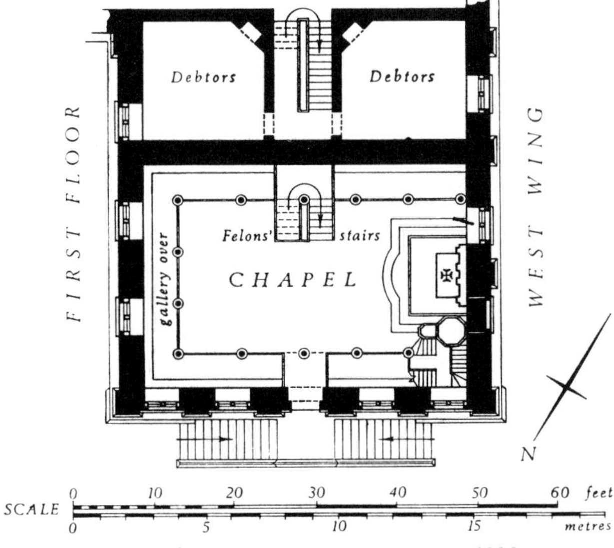

The Debtors' Prison: W. wing circa 1810

On the first floor the principal feature is a staircase in the centre of the main range resembling that in the E. wing. The Governor's parlour and under-gaoler's room in the E. wing are now a restaurant. The site of the chapel in the W. wing is now occupied by offices. The chapel originally rose through the first and second floors and could be reached by a passage and stairs from the court between the wings: the moulded plaster cornice around its walls is visible in rooms at second-floor level. It was described as 'handsome and beautiful . . . with Altar handsomly railed in, and the Pavement black and white marble, a decent Pulpit and all the Furniture of it answerable'.[1] There was a gallery supported on free-standing columns for the warders, debtors, and visitors; women sat in the centre with the felons and convicts around the walls. The altar was against the W. wall with the pulpit to the N.[2] (Fig. p. 81 after plan in Brierley drawings).

On the second floor the central staircase continues in a simpler form. The corridor in the main E.–W. range has plastered vaults with a circular opening below the turret. The hipped lead roofs were extensively restored in 1959.

Fittings: The communion plate provided for the prison chapel consisted in 1726 of a large chalice, a lesser chalice with cover, a large and a small salver, all of silver, and a pewter flagon.[3] Of these there remain at St. Hilda's church, Tang Hall, York, a cup with cover paten and a salver (Pl. 15), both made by John Langwith of York in 1703, inscribed as belonging 'to the Chappel in the Castle in the County of York' and dated '1706'. Also with these is a 19th-century flagon from the castle chapel. Another cup, dated 1673, was made in 1672 by John Thompson of York, but had disappeared by 1913.[4]

The 'King's Plate' was a collection of fetters and weapons once exhibited in the jailer's office at the prison and later, in part, at the Yorkshire Museum.[5] Only two 18th-century leg irons remain in the Castle Museum, one of them reputedly worn by Dick Turpin in 1739.

The clock works, housed in a room at the base of the turret and reached by an original ladder, have been much altered. Brass plates record the original installation (IOHN TERRY YORK FECIT 1716) and details of modifications by George Blakeborough in 1854 and

[1] Torr, 150. [2] Hargrove, II, 238. [3] NR Rec. Soc., VIII, 175. [4] T. M. Fallow and H. B. McCall, *Yorkshire Church Plate*, I (1912), 5–6.

[5] Sheahan and Whellan, 625; A. W. Twyford and A. Griffiths, *Records of York Castle* (1880), 168; *YMH*, 188.

G. J. Newey in 1902. The bell in the octagonal turret above is dated 1716.

THE ASSIZE COURTS (Pls. 10–13, 16; Figs. pp. 83, 84), of two storeys with basement, has walls of stone in the main façade to the E. and of brick with stone dressings elsewhere. The roofs are covered with Westmorland and some Welsh slates.

This Court House or 'Basilica' was erected in 1773–7 to designs by John Carr which were prepared as early as 1765.[1] Later alterations and additions have been made to provide more accommodation in the two Courts and to enlarge the attached offices. In 1812 Peter Atkinson senior added larger galleries in the Courts and access staircases at the outer ends of the front lobbies. Peter Atkinson junior and his partner Matthew Philips remodelled rooms on the W. in 1818, and by 1821 the main range on that side had been rebuilt much as it now stands. Atkinson and his later partner R. H. Sharp produced designs which included alteration of the entrance hall and addition of a *porte cochère*, but under this scheme only a new magistrates' room had been completed by 1824. After 1835 P. F. Robinson and G. T. Andrews remodelled galleries in the Crown Court and designed staircases and a stone screen in the entrance hall. The podium and lower flight of steps on the main front were added at about this time (drawings in Brierley collection). In *c.* 1870 I. Gould and C. Fisher built the High Sheriff's Luncheon Room and the County Committee Room on the S.W. A two-storey range at the N. end containing the house of the Keeper of the Courts was added in 1937, and in recent years restoration of the seating, redecoration, and reconstruction of the portico have been carried out by Messrs. Ward, Ruddick, and Ward. The building is a fine example of Carr's work, in his home city.

Architectural Description. The E. front, faced in fine-grained Ackworth sandstone, has a portico of four plain Ionic columns *in antis* freestanding between Ionic pilasters flanked on each side by three plain bays and then an outermost bay with attached Ionic columns *in antis*. All along the front is a plain square plinth, a string with guilloche ornament between the storeys, and an entablature with a modillion-cornice and plain frieze. The parapet, in part pierced and balustraded, has a moulded capping. In the pediment above the portico is a finely carved wreath with fasces and a staff crossed in saltire; on the end of the staff is a cap of liberty. The Shire Hall at Nottingham (1770) and the Sessions House at Canterbury (1806) have similar devices in their pediments. On the apex of the pediment stands a figure of Justice with scales and spear ('Mother Justice tall and thin, Who never yet hath ventured in');[2] couchant on the flanking lengths of parapet are a lion (l) and unicorn (r), both facing outward. The portico, approached up two broad flights of stone steps, has in the recessed back wall three round-headed wall-arches, each with a moulded architrave to the arch and moulded imposts; the central archway contains a two-leaf door below a fanlight, and both the others contain sash windows. Over them and above the string with guilloche enrichment are three round windows each with a moulded architrave and containing radial glazing. The N. and S. end walls of the recessed entry have each a round-headed archway fitted with an iron grille at ground-floor level.

The lower windows of the plain flanking bays are round-headed and the upper ones square. The outermost columniated bays have windows resembling those in the portico and in the centre of the parapet over each is a broad pedestal-block with a recessed panel carved with a garland and supporting a large urn. The comparatively plain single-storey annexes on each end are additions, of 1818 to the S. and 1937 to the N.

The N. and S. ends of the main block are of brick with rusticated stone quoins. The roofs are of Westmorland slate with lead flashing, and the simple conical glazed cupola over each Court is original.

The W. side of 1818 is of brick rendered in Roman cement and has a three-sided bay window near the middle with four bays to the N. and seven to the S. The high basement has a few heavily barred windows; there are bands at sill level of both ground and first-floor windows and a moulded stone cornice. The windows have moulded architraves, cornices, and sills, these last of the taller lower windows being supported by two consoles; all these elaborations are in cement. A block of 1821 projecting S. of the 1818 S. annexe has a basement faced in magnesian limestone and three barred round-headed windows on the W. and one on the S. Above these windows the wall is similar to that of the rest of the W. side, with a moulded cornice. The roof, hipped to the S., is of Welsh slate with lead flashing.

Inside, the entrance hall and the two Courts on the ground or main floor rise through the full height of the

[1] *YAJ*, IV, 205; W. A. Papworth (ed), *The Dictionary of Architecture* (1853–96), II, 36.

[2] J. Montgomery, *Prison Amusements*, 149.

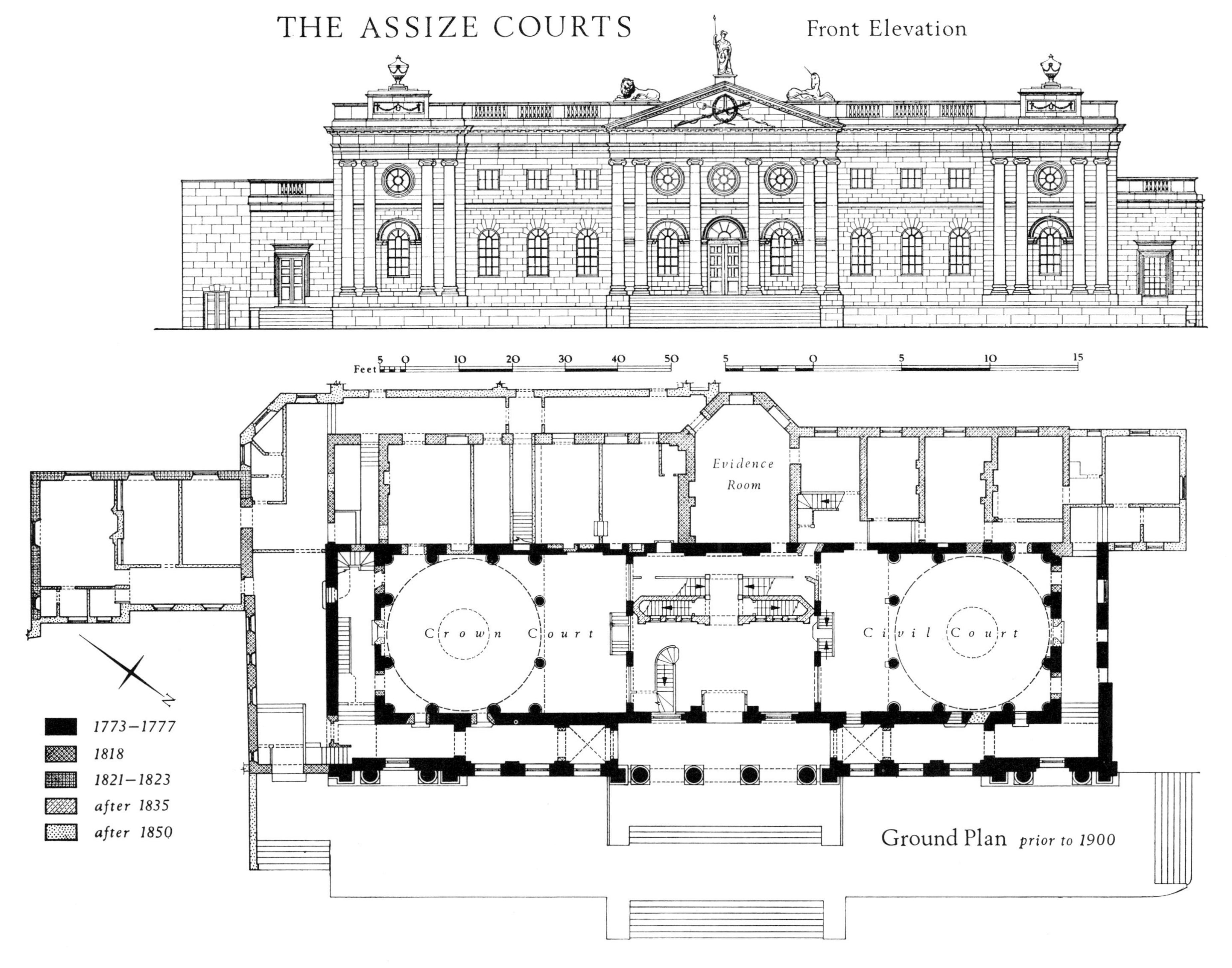
THE ASSIZE COURTS
Front Elevation
Feet 5 0 10 20 30 40 50
5 0 5 10 15
Evidence Room
Crown Court
Civil Court
N
1773–1777
1818
1821–1823
after 1835
after 1850
Ground Plan prior to 1900

York Castle. Plasterwork of the Civil Court Dome.

building. The *Entrance Hall* has an enriched dentil-cornice with a frieze decorated with lions' heads set on marigolds between triglyphs. The N. and S. walls have three round-headed archways, all but two containing door-ways, below round windows. The E. wall is similar but the central bay projects and has a large round-headed recess embracing the main entrance door-way and the window above it. A glazed internal porch has been added here. The appearance of the hall has been encumbered by the stone screen to the W., inserted in 1835 to conceal stairways to the galleries, and by a third staircase added against the S. wall. The screen has a central square-headed opening framed by pilasters below a pair of consoles and flanked by round-headed windows. The staircases have moulded rails and cast-iron balusters.

The two Courts are of similar rectangular plan but differ in detail. The *Civil Court* on the N. is the more ornate (Pl. 11). Over the N. part is a dome supported on eight unfluted columns plastered and painted to imitate green marble, with gilded capitals (Pl. 12), moulded bases, and tall plinths; they are an individual variant of the Corinthian order. Two are freestanding and the rest together with four in the angles outside the dome are engaged. The dome (Pl. 13; Fig. adjacent) springs from an entablature with elaborate cornice and a frieze with torch standards, festoons, and pelta-shaped decoration and rises to a band of urns and honeysuckle below the glazed cupola; the sides between have shallow projecting ribs decorated with guilloche, between which are swags, festoons, and other enrichments. In each spandrel of the ceiling is a medallion consisting of a central marigold with fluting radiating to a band of guilloche. The present colour scheme of the plasterwork in pink and white is by Cecil Ward. The walls are wainscotted with oak fielded panels below a fluted frieze and enriched cornice. Some panels are original, but in the N. wall the three doorways are of *c.* 1820. The added galleries with balustrades have been formed in rooms and corridors of the original building and the intervening walls pierced by segmental arches.

The *Crown Court* (Pl. 10) resembles the Civil Court but the dome has fewer ribs, the frieze below has foliated paterae set against crossed fasces and falchions and the columns are painted to resemble yellow marble. The cast-iron railings to the galleries on three sides of the Court, decorated with fasces and lions' masks, are of 1835–40. The oak panelling and much of the seating is

THE FEMALE PRISON, YORK CASTLE

Before conversion to Castle Museum

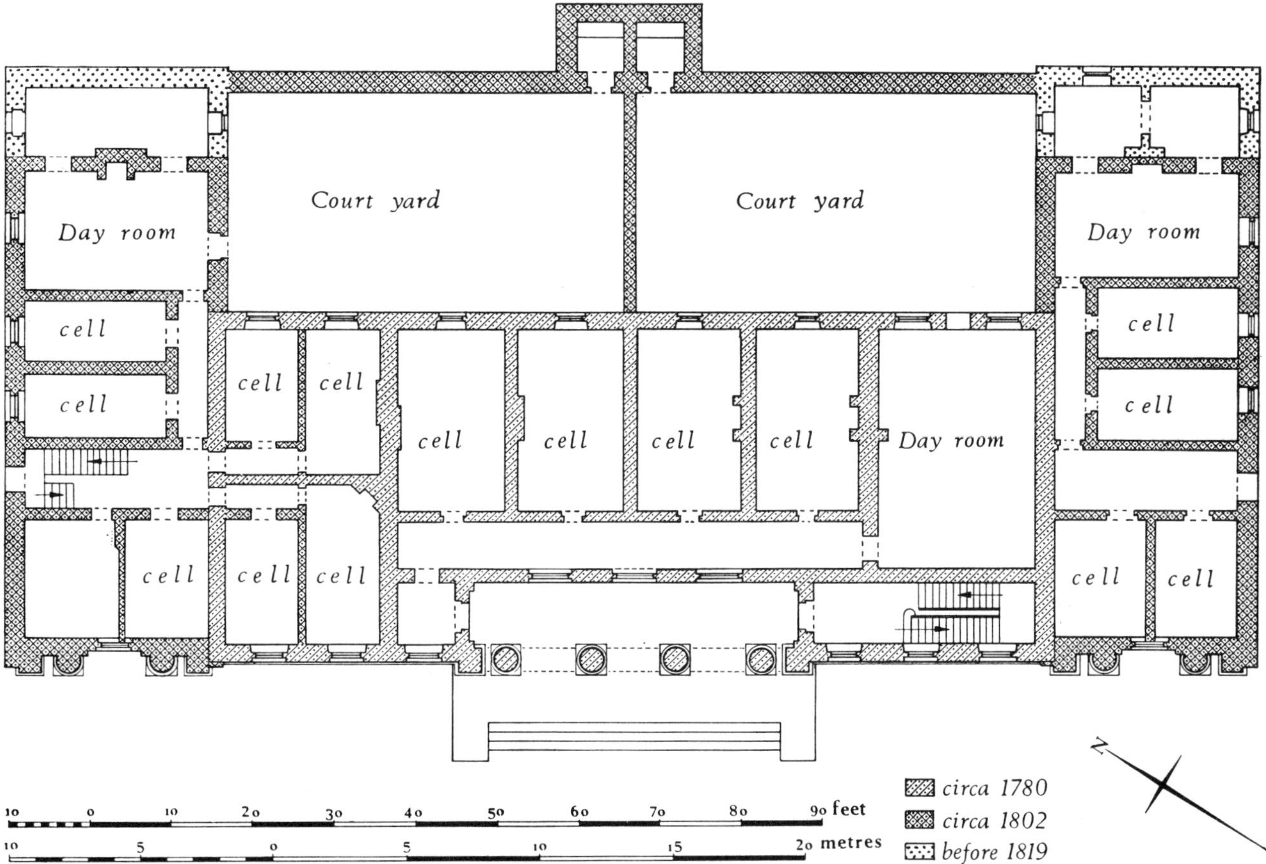

original although rearranged; the royal arms over the Judge's seat of *c.* 1840 are signed IW for John Wolstenholme.

Of the other rooms on this floor the Evidence Room at the centre of the W. block has a fireplace in a plain marble surround with a Carron cast-iron grate with female figures and rabbits in oval medallions.

In the basement, cell doors said to come from the Debtors' Prison have feeding hatches and cast-iron plates by C. Smith & Sons, Deritend Bridge Works, Birmingham.

THE FEMALE PRISON (Pl. 16; Fig. above), of two storeys, has walls of stone and brick and slate-covered or glazed roofs.

Tenders for a new building to replace the Moot Hall were invited in March 1779. A design by Thomas Wilkinson and John Prince, preferred to those of Richard Raisin and William Shepherd, was approved on 4 May. The work was to cost £1540. The central part of the building was erected in 1780–3 under the direction of John Carr; its front matches that of the Assize Courts opposite.[1] The wings were added, again matching on the W. the end bays of the Assize Courts, and other alterations were made in 1802 by Peter Atkinson senior. As at the Assize Courts, the podium and lower flight of steps were added between 1820 and 1850. In 1934 the prison was bought by York Corporation and drastically modified to house the Kirk Collections of bygones. It was opened as the Castle Museum in 1938. In the old exercise yards to the E. the street façades of 'Kirkgate' and 'Alderman's Walk' have been formed as museum

[1] North Riding County Record Office: QSM 2/26, 130, 147, 166, 175, 176; *York Courant*, 27 Oct. 1778, 2 Feb., 16 Mar. 1779. Drake, 1785 ed., III Addendum to II, 298; 1788 ed., pl. opp. 26.

exhibits; they incorporate reerected façades and fragments from York and other towns.

Architectural Description. The W. side, faced in sandstone, has a central tetrastyle portico of the Ionic order fronting a recessed entry and flanked on each side by three plain bays and pavilion-like end bays with attached Ionic columns, all the columns being *in antis*. In these and most other respects the design is similar to that of the Assize Courts opposite (*see* foregoing entry). Exceptions are the pierced and grilled lunettes in the three round-headed wall-arches of the back wall of the portico, the words 'CASTLE MUSEUM' in metal letters added on the frieze of the main entablature, and the omission or loss of the carved figures, urns, etc. on the main parapet and in the tympanum of the pediment of the portico. As noted, the columniated end bays are additions.

The N. end is cement-rendered and with simple cell windows protected with iron grilles on three levels, and in the centre of the ground floor is a large opening with glazed double doors. The S. end is mostly concealed by a single-storey stone-built addition, formerly a wash-house, but above this it is of brick with an ashlar entablature and brick parapet with stone coping. The brick E. side has been considerably altered for one side of 'Kirkgate', but some original windows remain.

The interior has been so modified for the museum that most surviving original features are concealed. Originally the ground floor was divided into cells for women felons and the upper floor into more comfortable rooms for debtors, but both had offices in the N. wing where a chapel was later formed. The plain staircases, cell doors in the corridor below the portico, and stone flagging in the former chapel on the first floor, with signs of the altar rail setting, are still visible.

The 'Kirkgate' exhibit includes the entrance to a reconstructed tallow-dip factory which incorporates the iron-bound gate with wicket and, above, the royal arms of George IV, signed PURDY, LONDON (Pl. 4), both from the main Castle gate to Tower Street of 1825–35. The fireplace and panelling from the court room on the first floor of the gatehouse is now in the bar of the Masons' Arms public house, Fishergate (Pl. 15).

Remains of other York buildings in 'Kirkgate' include late 18th-century windows from no. 9 St. Saviourgate ('Wilson and Goodall'), an 18th-century porch from Little Stonegate, and 19th-century windows from no. 2 Minster Gates ('William Whincup').[1]

[1] York Corporation, *The Parish of York Castle* (n.d.).

CLIFFORD'S TOWER IN THE 17TH CENTURY

Among the manuscripts belonging to the Earl of Dartmouth is a large folio volume[1] containing a detailed report on the state of Clifford's Tower and York Castle made in 1682 by Sir Christopher Musgrave to Colonel George Legge, Master-General of the Ordnance, created first Baron Dartmouth later that year.[2] Since the plans illustrating this report are dated 1685, and since there is a second report made in 1684 after the fire in Clifford's Tower, the manuscript is probably a fair copy prepared for reference purposes in 1685 and retained with other official Ordnance papers by Lord Dartmouth.

The main report, dated 16 November 1682, is the result of a visit to York made on 18–19 October and mentioned in his memoirs by Sir John Reresby.[3] Musgrave was accompanied by Martin Beckman, at that time Second Engineer of Great Britain,[4] who presumably drew the original plans referred to in the text. However, the three plans accompanying the report, of the King's Manor, the Castle (Pl. 62), and the whole city (Pl. 61), are signed by Jacob Richards.[5] The plan of the city, apart from execution in several colours and greater elaboration and arrangement of the keys, is substantially identical with that in York City Library signed by James Archer (Pl. 60). It is uncertain whether the latter was drawn by Captain James Archer senior, a Catholic Irishman, who made a survey of Castle Cornet, Guernsey, in 1673, worked on fortifications at Kinsale in 1678, and had died by January 1681,[6] or by his son Captain James Archer junior,[7] whether it was made on the occasion of Musgrave's visit or whether both it and Richards' plan of York are copies of a lost original. Probably Beckman prepared plans for Musgrave in 1682, Richards copied these in 1685 soon after his appointment to the Ordnance Office, but James Archer senior made the York Library copy, some ten years earlier, perhaps for Charles II since it was 'by His Majesty's speciall command'. It could then have left the King's possession at or after the revolution of 1688. The bastions around the Castle shown on the plans are, as the text makes clear, part of Beckman's suggestions for modernising its defences.

Musgrave's report starts by reciting Charles II's commission to Legge, dated 1 May 1682, to survey all magazines, castles and forts in England and then quotes Legge's warrant to himself: 'to goe to inspect and survey the Castle of York and Clifford's Tower and to take to my assistance Major Martin Beckman, one of His Majesty's Engineers, and to take an Account of the State of the Fortifications and Repairs of the said Garrison, as likewise of the Governor, Officers and Soldiers, and their severall Entertainements, and alsoe to take an exact Account of all the Ordnance Carriages, Munition and Habilliaments of Warr in the second place, and generally that I should consider of, and Certifie all other Particulars which I should find most advantageous to His Majesty's service touching the said Citty, Castle, and Tower'.

He then quotes Reresby's warrant of appointment as Governor, and gives his pay as £500 per annum. Successive paragraphs deal with the garrison, an infantry company of which the Earl of Mulgrave was Colonel and John Bristow was Captain Lieutenant, their annual pay of £1009. 16*s*. 8*d*., the master gunner and storekeeper Edward Baldock, the allowance for fire and candles, the duties of the garrison (one guard of seven men in the Thursday Market and one of four men in Clifford's Tower) and the absence of guards at the city gates. The condition of the King's Manor is summarised and there are a muster roll of the garrison and detailed inventories of the furniture in the Manor and of the artillery and stores in the Tower (*see* p. 178). Many small arms are listed and a special section deals with arms taken from Papists. Beckman's estimates and costings for new work at the Tower and Castle are set out: the main expense would be on six new bastions. He

---

[1] Staffordshire County Record Office, Stafford: Dartmouth Manuscripts D1778/III/02. The Commissioners are grateful to Lord Dartmouth for his permission to quote from the MS. It came to their notice when the Inventory was going into page proof and, important though it is, has had therefore to be restricted to this appendix. Hist. MSS Com. XV, App. I (1896), *Dartmouth* III, 54.

[2] See *Dictionary of National Biography* under Musgrave, Christopher, and Legge, George.

[3] Browning, A. (ed), *Memoirs of Sir John Reresby* (1936), 279–80 and above p. 72.

[4] See *Dictionary of National Biography*, Supplement, 160–2.

[5] *ibid.* under Richards, Jacob, and *CSP: Dom. 1685*, no. 1357.

[6] *CSP*: *Dom. 1672–3*, 470, 510, 549; *1673–5*, 80–1; *1680–1*, 136; *1683–4*, 393. Hist. MSS Com. *Dartmouth* I, 20; *Ormonde* n.s. IV, 135, 189–90, 227, 260.

[7] *CSP*: *Dom. 1675–6*, 509; *1678*, 536; *1685*, 417.

proposed that, if only the Tower was strengthened, the Castle wall facing it should be taken down and replaced by palisades.

In his final paragraph Musgrave suggests that Hull, when completed, will be a sufficient magazine for the county, and that if another is needed Scarborough can be fitted out at little cost. He therefore recommends that, to save the considerable expense of maintaining a governor and troops at York, Clifford's Tower should be disgarrisoned and demolished. Beckman had also recommended that the city gates should be pulled down. The main part of the report, the description of the fortress and proposals for its modernisation, are given below.

'The Castle and Clifford's Tower are very well Scituated for that end (for which it is conceived) they were built, the Tower Commanding all parts of the Citty. Nothing but the Walls were Standing when the late Queen Mother Landed at Burlington, and at her Majesty's charge Timbers were brought upon the walls and severall Roomes made in which his Majesty's Stores are now Lodged.[1]

There is alsoe a Platforme made upon the Top of the Tower, which is Leaded and Covered with Plancks, and about 10 peeces of Ordnance may be planted upon itt. There is no Area in it, or place for drawing up any Men, or conveniency to dispose of Musquetteers to secure the place from Surprize. The Condition of this place at present is such as makes it of little or noe consideration to his Majestie. And to make it in any Sort Usefull to His Majestie the present Battlements being too thyn must be taken downe and a Parrapet of Stone raised of Six foot thick, and att the Bottome of the Tower another Parrapet must be rased of Stone, Six foot thick for Musquetteers in time of Service. A Moate to be made about the Mount (upon which the Tower is placed) Sixty foot broad and Nyne foot deep. It is now a dry Graft. Alsoe a Scarp and Counter Scarp of Stone is to be made Twelve foot high and Seaven foot thick at the Topp; the Foundation of which must by Pyled and Covered with Planck. The Plattforme upon the Tower to be made new, and alsoe a new Drawbridge. These works and Repaires according to the Estimate of Particulars (hereunto annexed) made by Major Beckman Amount to the summe of £6174 besides the Charge of Purchaseing severall Gardens and Summer-houses for enlargeing the Moate, which the Citty layes claime to, and hath disposed of them to severall persons. But Clifford's Tower can never be well Defended and Supported but by Fortifieing the Castle, which ought to be the Maine Body of the Worke and the Tower onely an Out-worke to the Castle.

The Castle is not within the Liberty of the Citty, but in the County, and not under the Command of the Governor, who cannot passe to the Tower but through the Castle Yard, which is a large peece of Ground, in which is Built a large Court-house for the Judges to keep the Assizes in, And this was Rebuilt in the Yeare 1673, at the Countryes charge, and, as I am informed, they had his Majestie's leave to Rebuild Itt. This Building cost about £900. There is alsoe a handsome Building made for the Grand-Juries to be in att the Assizes, which cost the Country about £400. There are also severall houses in which the Sherriff keeps his Prisoners, The Castle being the County Goale.

To put this Castle into a Condition of Defence and Strength Six whole Bastions ought to be Erected, which together with Building Barracks for Soldiers, and Storehouses requisite for such a Fortification will cost according to Major Beckman's Estimate of the Particulars (hereunto Annex't) £29773. 10*s*.: And the Charge of Fortifieing the Tower being £6174: Amounts in all to the Sume of £35907. 10*s*. and the General fault of Estimates is to fall short not exceed.'

A supplementary report dated 12 November 1684 was made after a visit by Musgrave on 21 July to investigate the damage caused by the fire of 23 April 1684. He 'found that the Late Fire hath Burnt all the Tower except the Walls, which are Crack't, in some places from Topp to Bottome'. He had had the rubbish cleared away in order to find any stores buried in the ruins, had arranged for the weighing of lead and iron, and had had fallen bricks stacked against the inside walls of the tower. An appendix compares the stores catalogued in 1682, those issued since, those found still existing in 1684 and those destroyed. The first and last columns of this are printed below, being simplified by omitting the classifications of serviceable, repairable and unserviceable (*see* p. 178). Since the fire had left only the shell of the tower Musgrave again recommended it to be in the king's interest 'to demolish the same and sell the stones'.

In February 1683 Sir John Reresby had met Lord Dartmouth in Whitehall Palace and discussed with him the situation at York.[2] Dartmouth said that 'he was sorry he could not come down himselfe to take a vewe of the condition of Yorke but sent down the next to

---

[1] This statement confirms that in Torr, p. 105, and shows that the correct date for the restoration of the Tower during the Civil War is 1643 not 1642 as stated above pp. 22, 64. Queen Henrietta Maria was in York from 7 March to 6 June 1643. The year 1642 was thought more probable since the Earl of Cumberland's arms are on the forebuilding and the fifth and last earl was replaced at York late in 1642 and died without a male heir in 1643. Some have ascribed the 17th-century work in the forebuilding to a period after the siege.

[2] Browning, *op. cit.*, 290–1.

himselfe, which was Sir Christofer Musgrave, who had made a state of it and soe represented it that it could not be putt into a condition defensible for soe great a place under the charge of 30,000 l.; that the king had therefore resolved to reduce it'. It is now clear that the figure of £30,000 mentioned by Dartmouth was taken from Musgrave's report. Reresby replied that even if it would be too expensive to strengthen the city and castle defences 'the Tower, which commanded the whole citty, might be made very defensible for a small charge'. Lord Halifax then came up with the king and joined in the conversation. In the end Reresby was kept as Governor of York and the garrison was maintained. Even if the gutting of Clifford's Tower in 1684 might have led to the removal of the troops, Charles II's death and the troubles of his brother's reign caused their retention and reinforcement until the revolution of 1688.

'A Remaine of all the Ordnance, Carriages, Powder, Shott and other Stores and Provisions of Warr at Clifford's Tower in His Majesty's Citty of York taken by the Honourable Sir Christopher Musgrave Knight, Lieutenant Generall of his Majesty's Ordnance the 19th October 1682 together with an Accompt of what Stores have been Expended since the said Remaine, and what have been preserved out of the Late Accidentall Fire there, whereby it may appeare what Losse His Majestie hath Sustained by the said Fire. Videlicet.

		Length (in feet)	Weight cwt.	qrs.	lbs.	
Iron Ordnance mounted on Ship Carriages	12 Pounders:— 1	10	34	2	—	
	Saker:— 1	7	14	—	15	
		4	8	2	—	per estimate
Serviceable	3 Pounders:— 2	4	8	2	—	per estimate
Iron Ordnance mounted on Ship Carriages.	Saker:— 1	4½	12	—	7	
	Ditto Hammered:— 1	5½	8	2	2	
	Minion:— 1	6	14	3	—	
		7	15	—	6	
	3 Pounders:— 3	6	14	2	—	
Unserviceable		6	13	2	7	
Brass Ordnance mounted on a Travelling Carriage	Falconett:— 1	2	1	2	—	per estimate
Iron Murderers mounted of 2 foot 9 inches each	Culvering bore:— 1		7	—	—	per estimate
	Saker bore:— 1		5	—	—	per estimate

All the Carriages except two belonging to the aforesaid Gunns were destroyed by the Fire in the Tower, since which time the Gunns hereafter mencioned have been new Mounted by Order of Sir John Reresby Baronett Governor of his Majesty's Citty of York. Videlicet.[1]

	Length (in feet)	cwt.	qrs.	lbs.
Hammered Saker:— 1	5½	8	2	2
Minion:— 1	6	14	3	—
3 Pounder:— 1	7	15	—	6

	Remaine of Stores 19th October 1682	Stores lost by the Fire and Expended
Granado Shells for		
11 Inch	96	9
8½ Inch	34	2
7½ Inch	13	nil
7 Inch	23	12
Round Shott for		
Cannon (of) 7	1	1
Demy Cannon	147	nil

[1] Reresby wrote to Dartmouth in September 1687 hoping that the '5 small guns which he has remounted at his own charge, and planted upon the Tower hill, may be continued' (Hist. MSS. Com. *Dartmouth* I, 134).

	Remaine of Stores 19th October 1682	Stores lost by the Fire and Expended
24 Pounders	55	nil
Culvering	215	nil
Demy Culvering	163	nil
Saker	46	nil
Falcon	113	nil
Tynn Cases (to be filled with Musquett Shott)	32 empty	32
Hand Granadoes	39	nil
Ladles and Spunges		
12 Pounders	1 spunge	1
Minion	1 iron ladle, 1 spunge	1. 1.
3 Pounders	1 spunge	1
Powder	7¼ Barrells	nil
Match	26 cwt. 3 qrs. 6 lb.	7 cwt. 1 qr. 11 lb.
Halberts	23	23
Long Pikes	63	63
Musquett Shott in Barrells	46 cwt.	25 cwt. 3 qr. 25 lb.
Aprons of Lead	9	9
Centinell Bell	1	1
Crowes of Iron	2	1
Coines	4	4
Formers small	3	3
Tanned Hydes	2	2
Wadhook	1	1
Hand Spikes	3	3
Powder hornes	1	1
Primeing Iron	1	1
Match Lock Musquetts	1031	952
Snap hance Musquetts	108	108
Ditto with Wheele Locks	26	26
Carbines	71	2
Ditto with Wheele Locks	28	24
Bandaliers	52 collers	52
Pistolls	61½ pairs	21½ pairs
Ditto with Wheele Locks	27 pairs	23 pairs
Carbine Shott in Boxes	5¼ cwt.	5¼ cwt.
Belts for Carbines	69	69
Swivells for Ditto	50	50
Spanners for Ditto	25	25
Holsters	107 pairs	107 pairs
Cartouch Boxes	16	16
Swords	130	130

	Remaine of Stores 19th October 1682	Stores lost by the Fire and Expended
Drumms	16	16
Wall peeces	2	nil
Colour Staves	4	4
Scaleing Ladders	27	27
Head-peeces	30	2
Backs and Breasts	120 of each	18
Bedsteads for Soldiers	6	6
Grates with 4 Barrs	2	nil
Grates with 3 Barrs	1	nil
Creels for Carrying Armes	4 pairs	4 pairs
Collers and Hames for Horse Harness	10	10
Packsadles	19	19
Gin and Gin Rope	1	1
Guard Bedds	3	3
Small Table	1	1
Small Copper fix't in the Wall	1	nil
Brass Shivers	3	nil

Stores remaineing

Musquett Barrells	1040
Pistoll Barrells	20
Lead pick't out of the Rubbish	72 cwt. 2 qrs.
Iron pick't out of the Rubbish	15 cwt. 4 lb.

Armes Received from Papists

	Remaine of Stores 19th October 1682	Stores lost by the Fire and Expended
Backs and Breasts	3	3
Head peeces	2	2
Holsters	2 pairs	2 pairs
Fowling peeces	17	17
Snaphance Musquetts	2	2
Carbines	1	1
Pistolls	7 pairs	7 pairs
Swords	39	39
Semiters	2	2
Silver Hilted Sword	1	nil
Halberts	2	2
Drumms	1	1.'

ABBREVIATIONS

Ant. J.	Antiquaries' Journal.
Arch. J.	Archaeological Journal.
BM	British Museum.
Bod. Lib.	Bodleian Library, Oxford.
CCR	Calendar of Close Rolls.
CIM	Calendar of Inquisitions Miscellaneous.
CLP	Calendar of Letters and Papers.
CLR	Calendar of Liberate Rolls.
CPR	Calendar of Patent Rolls.
CSP: Dom.	Calendar of State Papers, Domestic.
Cooper (1911)	Cooper, T. P., *The History of the Castle of York* (1911).
Drake	Drake, F., *Eboracum: History and Antiquities of the City of York* (1736).
Gents. Mag.	Gentleman's Magazine.
Hargrove	Hargrove, W., *History and Description of the Ancient City of York*, 3 vols. (1818).
Hist. MSS Com.	The Royal Commission on Historical Manuscripts.
King	King, E., 'Sequel to the Observations on Ancient Castles', *Archaeologia*, VI (1780), 259–60.
King's Works	Brown, R. A., Colvin, H. M. and Taylor, A. J., *History of the King's Works*, I, II, *The Middle Ages* (1963).
NG	National Grid, reference in 100-kilometre square SE.
NR Rec. Soc.	North Riding Record Society.
O'Neil (1934)	O'Neil, B. H. St. J. 'A note on the date of Clifford's Tower, York', *Arch. J.*, XCI (1934), 296–310.
O'Neil (1936)	*Clifford's Tower, York Castle* (1936).
„ (1939)	'Excavations at York Castle, 1935', *Ant. J.*, XIX (1939), 85–90.
Pressly	Pressly, I. P., *The Castle of York* (1950).
PRO	Public Record Office.
RCHM	The Royal Commission on Historical Monuments (England).
„ *York City*, I	City of York Inventory, vol. I. *Eburacum, Roman York* (1962).
Renn	Renn, D. F., *Clifford's Tower and the Castles of York* (1971).
RS	Rolls Series.
Salzman	Salzman, L. F., *Building in England down to 1540* (1967).
Sheahan and Whellan	Sheahan, J. J. and Whellan, T., *History and Topography of the City of York, the Ainsty Wapentake, and the East Riding of Yorkshire* (1855).
Slingsby, *Diary*	Parsons, D. (ed.) *The Diary of Sir Henry Slingsby of Scriven, Bart.* (1836).
Taylor	Taylor, A. J., 'The Date of Clifford's Tower', *Arch. J.*, CXI (1954), 153–9.
Torr	Torr. J., *The Antiquities of York City* (1719).
VCH, *York*	Victoria County History, *The City of York* (1961).
YAJ	Yorkshire Archaeological Journal.
YASRS	Yorkshire Archaeological Society Record Series.
YPSR	Yorkshire Philosophical Society, *Annual Reports*.

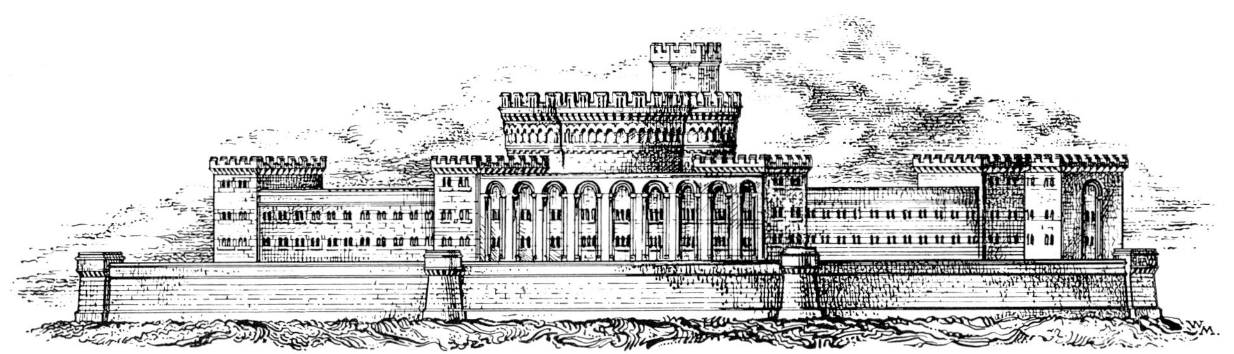

PROJECTED NORTH-WEST ELEVATION OF YORK CASTLE, AFTER ROBERT WALLACE, 1824

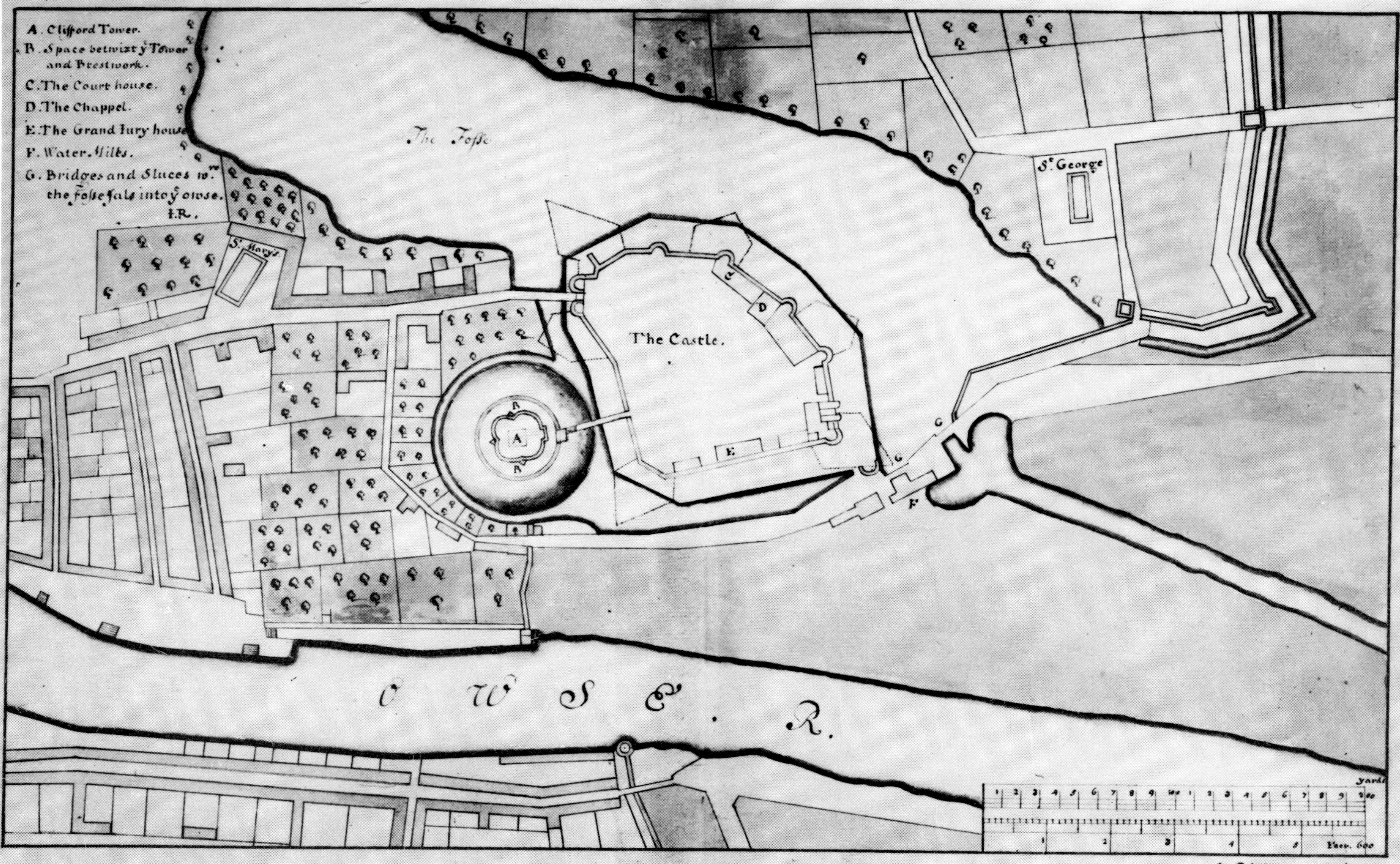

PLATE 62. YORK CASTLE. Plan, drawing by Jacob Richards, 1685.